D0777174

"And Then Tiger Told the Shark..."

"And Then Tiger Told the Shark..."

A Collection of the Greatest True Golf Stories of All Time

DON WADE

Foreword by Sam Snead

CONTEMPORARY BOOKS

Library of Congress Cataloging-in-Publication Data

Wade, Don.
    "And then Tiger told the Shark . . ." : a collection of the greatest
true golf stories of all time / Don Wade ; foreword by Sam Snead.
      p.   cm.
    ISBN 0-8092-2799-1
    1. Golf—Anecdotes.   2. Golf—Humor.   I. Title.
GV967.W27   1999
796.352—dc21   98-33215
                                                          CIP

Cover design by Todd Petersen
Jacket front photograph copyright © 1998 Stephen Szurlej
Illustrations by Paul Szep

Published by Contemporary Books
A division of NTC/Contemporary Publishing Group, Inc.
4255 West Touhy Avenue, Lincolnwood (Chicago), Illinois 60646-1975
U.S.A.
Copyright © 2000 by Don Wade
Printed in the United States of America
International Standard Book Number: 0-8092-2799-1
99 00 01 02 03 04 LB 17 16 15 14 13 12 11 10 9 8 7 6 5 4 3 2 1

This one's for all the people who make
this such a special game.

CONTENTS

FOREWORD

I first met Don Wade back in 1978, when he was just starting as an editor at *Golf Digest*. In fact, I was the subject of the first story he ever did for the magazine.

Gardner Dickinson and I had just won the first Legends of Golf, and Don came down to Pinehurst, where I was giving playing lessons for the *Golf Digest* Schools.

I've been giving him lessons ever since.

Over the years, Don and I have done any number of magazine articles together, and we collaborated on an instruction book that's been in the stores since 1989. In all those years, whenever we'd get together to work on a story, we'd find time to play—and he was always a quick study.

Fortunately, not quick enough to become expensive, but we've had a lot of fun, and we've even teamed up to pluck a few pigeons over the years.

What always impressed me about Don was that he loved to listen to stories about the years I spent on the Tour. He's always had a good ear for a story, and that's been proven by the success this series of books has enjoyed. When the first book, *"And Then Jack Said to Arnie . . ."*, came out, I told him I was glad he finally put all those stories I've been telling him to good use. He's managed to get some of these stories

in each of the six books that have followed, and I've enjoyed reading every one of them.

I'm also glad that he asked me to write this Foreword because this book, like all the other's in Don's series, really captures the flavor of the game.

If you love golf, you'll love this book.

Good luck and good golfing!

—Sam Snead

ACKNOWLEDGMENTS

This book, like the others in the series that began with *"And Then Jack Said to Arnie . . ."* in 1991, is really a team effort, and I'd like to thank the people who are part of the team.

Paul Szep is a two-time Pulitzer Prize–winning editorial cartoonist for the *Boston Globe*. His illustrations are a big reason these books have been successful. When you study his drawings, you see the work of not only an extraordinary artist but a guy who truly loves the game of golf. That he also happens to be a great friend just makes it so much the better. Thanks, Szeppy.

It is a measure of Steve Szurlej's talent that when he was given the job of shooting the cover for *"And Then Jack Said to Arnie . . ."*, we didn't bother to give him any suggestions. He didn't need any. That cover, and the covers that followed, captured an important part of the game—friendships that are born in competition and last throughout the years.

Nancy Crossman was the editor who bought the first book and supported this series for the last several years. When she left NTC/Contemporary to strike out on her own, Matthew Carnicelli took over, and he's been terrific. He's been supportive, he's been skillful, and most important, he's kept his sense of humor about the whole business.

Just as this book was being finished, my longtime and long-suffering agent, Chris Tomasino, decided to leave the agency and fly solo. Thanks to her for all she's done for all these years, but most especially, thanks for her unfailing friendship. Now the care and nurturing of my writing career falls to Jonathan Diamond—and for that, I'm thankful as well.

Thanks to the writers, players, readers, and "Golf Guys" who have been so generous in sharing their stories. Keep them coming.

And special thanks to Sam Snead for writing the Foreword for this book. Sam and I go back more than 20 years. I did my first story for *Golf Digest* with him, and he's been a dear friend ever since. Many of my fondest memories in golf are of my time with Sam. Thanks for everything.

ARCHITECTS

When celebrated golf course architect Pete Dye was first approached about designing the Tournament Players Club at Sawgrass, he was skeptical. Actually, that's putting it mildly. The site was literally a swamp, and even a person with Dye's considerable imagination had difficulty envisioning a golf course ever emerging from the mire.

But then-PGA Tour Commissioner Deane Beman was a man who was nothing if not determined—and persuasive. He and Vernon Kelly, the property manager, brought Dye to Ponte Vedra Beach to tour the property.

The three men went around and around the site, with Kelly pointing out high, dry ground that would make excellent hole locations. After a while, Dye began to see the course taking shape in his mind's eye.

"It wasn't until I actually started designing the course that I realized they had been leading me around to the same patch of dry ground," Dye later joked. "It was the only dry ground out there."

Pete Dye has never taken himself or his work all that seriously. In fact, he's able to joke about his qualifications.

"My father designed a nine-hole course in Urbana, Ohio, and it's a good one, too," Dye once said. "He built it in 1923, and at that time he'd only been playing golf for about two years. That shows you how much you need to know about golf to build a course."

Incidentally, seventy years after the first nine was built, Pete's son, P.B., built a second nine.

"Urbana is a pretty conservative town," Pete said. "I guess they just wanted to wait and make sure this golf stuff was really going to catch on before they went ahead and spent any more money."

Donald Ross was born and raised in Dornach, Scotland, and his religious roots ran deep. One day a writer ran into Ross and praised him for his brilliant masterpiece, Pinehurst #2.

Ross thanked him—and then corrected him.

"God created those holes," Ross said. "All I did was discover them."

On another occasion, he famously summoned the Almighty while surveying the property where he would design the South Course at Oakland Hills near Detroit. He climbed a slight slope and gazed down upon what are now the 10th and 11th holes.

"God intended this to be a golf course," he said, no doubt to the considerable relief of the club's founders, who had not only Ross but the Lord Himself on their side.

Robert Trent Jones is widely credited with making golf course design a big business. Indeed, with more than four hundred courses to his credit, no architect has ever been more prolific. At last count, Jones has designed courses in forty-three states and thirty-four countries, and in doing so, he has helped popularize the game immeasurably.

In celebration of his career, Jones was named to the World Golf Hall of Fame. He was there for the opening ceremonies in 1998, although at age ninety-two, he was largely restricted to a wheelchair.

As the other members of the Hall of Fame gathered before appearing onstage, a well-meaning volunteer asked a gentleman standing nearby if he'd mind pushing Jones to the elevator and taking him up to the stage level.

"I'd be happy to," said a gracious, if slightly bemused, Arnold Palmer.

Ben Hogan is believed to have designed just one course, the Trophy Club, near Houston. But he ended his involvement following a dispute with the developers.

In the 1960s, however, he was asked to redesign a string of holes at Colonial. Hogan thought the problem was that some trees had become overgrown, so he did the only logical thing: he called in the chain saws.

Not surprisingly, perhaps, this was more than the club's members had in mind.

Ben Hogan or no Ben Hogan, they ordered the cutting stopped. Hogan complied . . . and quit the project cold.

3

AUGUSTA NATIONAL GOLF CLUB

Until 1990, when Ron Townsend became the first African-American member of Augusta National, the club had been widely criticized for the lack of diversity among its membership. Even a few years later, members would occasionally make embarrassing faux pas when it came to the matter of race.

In 1995, there was a lot of speculation concerning how Tiger Woods, then the U.S. Amateur champion, would fare at the Masters. A longtime Augusta member was standing near the clubhouse when a tall, dark-skinned player approached.

"Hello," said the member, extending his hand. "You must be Tiger Woods. We've heard a lot about you, and I want to personally welcome you here to Augusta National and the Masters."

"No, sir," said the player, shaking the man's hand. "I'm Vijay Singh from Fiji."

The Masters is arguably the world's best-run tournament, but in the early days it was very much a club affair, overseen by the club's legendary chairman, Clifford Roberts.

"We didn't have rules officials like we do today, so members would often make the rulings," remembers longtime member Charlie Yates. "One year, we'd had a lot of rain, and Cliff thought we might need some rulings down around 11 and 12. He asked Bob Jones's father, the Colonel, to wander on down there in case there were any problems.

"Sure enough, the Colonel hadn't been down there very long, before a player had a ball plug near the pond on the 12th green. There was a question whether it was in the hazard or whether he was allowed relief. The Colonel studied the situation but really wasn't sure about what was the right decision. Finally, he asked the player how he stood.

"Four over for today and 17 over for the tournament," the man said.

"What difference does it make?" the Colonel said. "Go ahead and put the son of a bitch on the green if you want."

Even his friends used words like "stern" and "autocratic" to describe Cliff Roberts, but the bottom line was that he loved Augusta National and the Masters and was willing to do whatever he thought best to improve both the club and the tournament that made it famous.

During one Masters, Roberts walked up toward the clubhouse and started through the front door. He was stopped by an imposing security guard.

"Excuse me, sir, do you have a badge?" the guard asked.

"I'm Clifford Roberts," he said and started to walk around the guard, who again blocked his path.

"Yes, Mr. Roberts, but do you have a badge?" the guard said firmly but politely.

"You don't seem to understand," Roberts said icily. "I'm Clifford Roberts."

"Yes, Mr. Roberts," the guard said. "I understand that, but do you have a badge? If you do, I'll be happy to let you into the clubhouse."

With that, Roberts turned and walked back to his cabin. He returned a few minutes later with his badge and showed it to the guard.

"Yes sir, Mr. Roberts," the guard said as he opened the door. "Thank you very much, and you have a nice day."

Roberts stared at the man, his face pinched and his eyes narrowing.

"What's your name?" Roberts demanded.

The guard answered, no doubt with more than a little nervousness in his voice.

"Fine," Roberts said as he walked past the man. "This job is yours for as long as you want it."

One of the traditions at the Masters is that the defending champion selects the menu for the annual Champions Dinner. In recent years, the choices have been haggis, a Scottish dish that can only be described as an acquired taste (Sandy Lyle in 1989); steak-and-kidney pie and fish and chips (Nick Faldo in 1991 and 1997); and chicken cacciatore (Fred Couples in 1993).

7

When Clifford Roberts was alive, however, the menu tended to reflect his tastes, which is to say it usually featured some variation on a strip steak dinner.

There was a reason for that.

"My first Champions Dinner was in 1964," Jack Nicklaus remembers. "The head waiter told me, 'Mr. Roberts likes this, and he likes to have that, and I think you'd probably like it, too.' I told him that if it was good enough for Mr. Roberts it was fine with me, and we all had a very nice dinner. I don't remember what we ate, but I'm sure it was very nice."

Masters champions—by club policy they are never referred to as "past champions"—are allowed to play the course whenever they like. But there are certain limitations, as Arnold Palmer found out when he brought his father, Deacon, down to play after his 1958 victory.

When they arrived, Cliff Roberts took Arnold aside and gave him the facts of life, so to speak, at Augusta National.

"Arnie, we're glad to have you play anytime you'd like, but your father can't play unless he has a member with him," Roberts said. "I'm afraid that's one of our rules."

Of course, it's fair to say that they didn't have a tough time scraping up a member to show the Palmers around the place.

On another occasion, Roberts even overruled Bob Jones when it came to a question of the club's rules.

One year, on the day after the Masters, some writers who were his close friends stopped by to see Jones. As their visit wound down, Jones invited the men to go out and play the virtually deserted par-3 course. As they were preparing to leave, Clifford Roberts arrived. When he learned of Jones's invitation, he begged to differ.

"Bob, surely you know the rule about guest play," he said. "All guests must play with a member."

Jones, confined to a wheelchair because of his illness, asked if an exception couldn't be made just this once. Roberts was not a man for making exceptions, especially when it came to the rules at Augusta National.

That left just one alternative. Roberts, who was recovering from surgery, would play with the writers.

Six holes later, he'd had enough and walked in, leaving the writers to finish unchaperoned.

Once again, history had been made at Augusta National.

AUSSIE RULES

The 1988 World Cup of Golf was played at Royal Melbourne, whose two wonderful courses were designed by Dr. Alister Mackenzie. The tournament attracted writers from around the world, who were naturally charmed by their Australian hosts.

One afternoon, as an American writer followed Ben Crenshaw—the eventual winner of the individual title—he fell into a conversation with a group of locals. Before long, they had extended an invitation for the American to join them at their club for a round of golf.

"Thanks a lot," the American said. "What time should I be there?"

"Oh, we don't play 'til after four or five," one of the Australians said.

"In the afternoon?" the American asked.

"No, mate," said another of the Australians. "Beers."

It's no secret that golf is a good way for businesses to promote their goods or services. But at the 1985 New South

Wales Open in Australia, a local official, Paul Smith, came up with a unique way to pick up a little publicity for his firm.

Mr. Smith sponsored a hole-in-one contest on a par 3. Anyone making an ace had a choice between winning £5,000 or a complete, prepaid send-off by Mr. Smith's highly regarded funeral home.

Talk about a decision that will weigh heavily on your mind.

SEVE BALLESTEROS

Seve Ballesteros is nothing if not an inventive scrambler. It's fair to say he can hit shots most other players can't even imagine. Very often, it's been the key to his success.

At the 1980 Masters, Seve hit a towering hook on the 17th hole that came to rest on the 7th green.

"Nice drive, Seve," joked David Graham, who was preparing to putt when Seve's ball bounced past. "Would you like to play through?"

Typical of Seve, he lofted a 7-iron over the bordering trees. The ball wound up fifteen feet from the hole, and he made a birdie.

He wound up winning his first Green Jacket by four strokes.

Seve has a particularly mischievous sense of humor," the late Peter Dobereiner once recalled. "One day I had happened to mention in my newspaper column that Seve was driving the ball wildly, even by his unusually erratic standards. That I had the statistics to prove this mattered little to Seve. The day the column appeared, he sought me out after his round to inform me that he had missed just two fairways, and those by merely the smallest of margins. These updates continued daily for what seemed like weeks, until he had made his point—with tiresome regularity."

CADDIES

A man and his longtime caddie were walking back to the clubhouse after the player had just been roundly trounced in the club championship.

"This is the worst beating I've ever had," the man said. "I'll never be able to lift my head around here again."

"I don't know, sir," the caddie said, trying to raise the man's spirits. "You had plenty of practice at it today."

For many years, the late Phil Harris, who was a fixture at the old Bing Crosby National Pro-Am, used to have a friend caddie for him. They were a perfect team, in large part because the caddie enjoyed taking a drink every bit as much as Phil did, and Phil always enjoyed the company of kindred spirits.

One morning they showed up for their early tee time, and it was hard to tell who was in worse shape. If anything, the nod probably went to Harris, who had to at least try to hit his

15

opening drive. All the caddie had to do was keep an eye on it—although in the end, even that proved to be too much for him to handle.

Harris wobbled to the tee and managed to get his ball on a peg without falling over. After steadying himself, he made a lurching swipe at the ball and somehow managed to make contact, however glancing.

"Where'd it go?" Harris asked his caddie.

"Where'd what go?" the caddie replied.

An American came to St. Andrews and was looking forward to the experience of hiring one of the caddies he had heard so many stories about. Sadly, the experience didn't work out quite as he'd hoped.

For starters, the caddie was particularly dour and his obvious hangover wasn't helping matters. Standing on the first tee, he took one look at the American's large bag and slowly shook his head.

"Did you nae leave anything at home?" he growled.

Trying to be accommodating, the American took out his rain jacket and extra sweater and left them in the clubhouse.

So off they went, but despite the caddie's advice, the man was clearly baffled by the mysteries of the Old Course. To make matters worse, storm clouds blew in off the water and it began to rain heavily.

"Here, I'll take the bag," the American said. "You go back to the clubhouse and get my rain jacket and sweater."

That was the last straw.

The caddie dropped the bag and glared at the American.

"Get it yourself," he said. "I'm a caddie not a bloody Rin Tin Tin that you can send to go fetch."

The caddies at Pine Valley are renowned for their remarkable ability to find shots that spray off into the course's abundant trees, shrubs, and waste areas.

One day a guest, playing in the fading twilight, hit a shot that sailed off into the gathering darkness.

"Did you see it?" he asked his caddie.

"No sir," the caddie said. "But it sounded pretty crooked to me."

Brad Faxon is a player who truly loves the game's traditions and its venerable old courses. Several years ago, he traveled to Scotland for the British Open, and while he was there, he took a side trip to Prestwick, the site of the first twelve British Opens. In fact, only Augusta National has hosted more major championships than Prestwick.

When he finished his round he asked his caddie, who had caddied there for decades, which was his favorite pub.

"The nearest one," the caddie said.

The Quaker Ridge Golf Club in Scarsdale, New York, is an A. W. Tillinghast masterpiece that is occasionally overshadowed by the thirty-six holes at its neighbor, Winged Foot. But Quaker Ridge can more than hold its own, as was evidenced when it hosted the 1997 Walker Cup matches, won by the United States.

Quaker Ridge can also hold its own when it comes to some of the characters they've had for caddies over the years.

One day, at an interclub match, one of the guests happened to be playing very well and made the turn at 1 under par. As he and his caddie headed to the 10th tee, the caddie decided it was time to tell the man just how impressed he was by his play.

"Man, I'm gonna start calling you 'Doc' because you've been operating on this course," the caddie said, no doubt figuring that such lavish praise couldn't hurt at the end of the round.

Bogey, bogey, bogey went his man over the next three holes.

"We need a birdie here," the man said to his caddie as they reached the tee on the long, par-3 13th.

"No, Doc," the caddie said, as he slowly and sadly shook his head. "What we need is some of that malpractice insurance."

Back in the 1930s, there was a member of the New Haven (Conn.) Country Club named F. L. Perry, who was by every account a lovely man and a passionate golfer.

Sadly, Mr. Perry had a difficult time walking and required the use of two canes just to get around. Since New Haven is a relatively hilly course, this made golf difficult—if not nearly impossible—for him in the days before golf carts.

One day, however, Mr. Perry came up with a brilliant solution to his problem: a rickshaw.

Now, just how he came up with the idea, not to mention how he found a rickshaw in New Haven, remains unclear. But suffice it to say, Mr. F. L. Perry was a very determined man.

Once he had his rickshaw, he found a caddie named Red Lawson, who was delighted to pull him around the course. And why not? For his efforts, he received his standard 75-cent caddie fee plus a whopping (for the time) 3 dollars for his work as a rickshaw driver.

CANTERBURY GOLF CLUB

Golf courses—even courses praised from their inception—are very often works in progress. That's true at Augusta National, for example, and it is certainly true at Cleveland's Canterbury Golf Club.

The course, which was started in 1922, was designed and built by Herbert Strong. No sooner was it up and running than architect Jack Way came in and made several changes. And there would be more along the way.

In 1932, Canterbury hosted the Western Open, and the members set out to take a serious look at their course. A very serious look.

Members were stationed on every hole and kept meticulous notes, trying to determine which holes were easy, which holes were hard, and which holes were simply unfair. Armed with their research, the club set out on a five-year program that saw thousands of trees planted, tees moved, bunkers added, and bunkers replaced. Having done all that, they changed it again on the eve of the 1940 U.S. Open.

So how good is Canterbury? Good enough to have hosted two U.S. Opens, two Western Opens, and a PGA Championship—and the members are still tinkering with the course.

JEANNE CARMEN

Jeanne Carmen wins the award for being the least likely person to ever appear in a collection of golf stories.

She was known as "the Queen of the B-Movies" for a string of films she made in the 1950s. To put it mildly, the films were short on plot, engaging dialogue, or acting that would ever be confused with the work of an Olivier or Hepburn.

They were, however, long on whatever sexual content the producers could get past censors at the time.

Jeanne Carmen was a model and actress who made her mark as a pinup girl in the late 1940s. She appeared in the pages—and often on the covers—of pulp men's magazines. She was a sort of Marilyn Monroe before the real Marilyn Monroe came along—an irony, since they became good friends.

In 1949, she took a job modeling golf clothes for a Los Angeles golf professional named Jack Redmond. It's worth noting that the clothes she modeled bore virtually no resemblance to what Patty Berg, Louise Suggs, Babe Zaharias, or any of the other top women players of the day wore—or could even imagine wearing.

On the day of the photo shoot, Redmond asked Carmen if

she played golf. Not surprisingly, she'd never touched a club until that day. Since they had some time to kill, he told her to go ahead and hit a ball into the net.

Since the club was for right-handed golfers and Ms. Carmen was a lefty, she did the only logical thing: she turned the club on its toe and hit the ball into the net so purely that the net crashed to the ground.

Jack Redmond watched her hit a few more shots and realized he had stumbled onto a gold mine. For the next six months he worked with her, teaching her every trick shot he knew. As it turned out, Jeanne Carmen had an incredible—even unbelievable—gift for the game. Add to that a genius for show business, and they were on their way.

"We would go on the road and do exhibitions," she said. "We'd do a half-hour exhibition and make $1,000. We were getting rich."

She was so skilled, she claims, that she could stand 150 yards from a flagpole and hit it on an average of once every three tries. The high point of their act was when Carmen would pick a man from the audience, have him lie on his back, and hit a ball teed up in his mouth.

Mercifully, she never hit a fat shot.

Everything was going along swimmingly until Jeanne Carmen's husband, an opera singer named Sandy Scott, began to get suspicious and decided to join them on the road. Not surprisingly, Scott and Redmond instantly detested one another. Finally, on a trip from Los Angeles to Florida, Redmond decided the money wasn't worth it, tossed them out of the car, and went on his way.

In the days that followed, the couple decided to get a divorce. Without a car, they were stuck until a man came along and offered a ride.

"Yes, thanks," said Scott.

"Not you," the man said. "Her."

As it happened, the man was a gangster named Johnny Rosselli, who would later be implicated in alleged CIA plots against Fidel Castro.

Since Mr. Rosselli had a certain animal charm about him—and more important—a car, Jeanne Carmen hopped in and they headed for Las Vegas, which under no circumstances should be confused with the Disneyesque version offered up for Middle American consumption today.

Johnny Rosselli's particular line of work surfaced early in their relationship.

"We got to Vegas, and as we drove down the strip, Johnny would point out the different hotels and casinos," said Carmen. "Then he'd shoot out one of the lights on their signs."

Whatever other attraction Jeanne Carmen held for Johnny Rosselli, he quickly came to appreciate her remarkable golf skills.

"Johnny would find wealthy hotel guests and set them up," she said. "He'd point to me and bet them they couldn't beat me. I'd start slowly and let them get ahead for the first five or six holes, then I'd make this amazing improvement. I never lost."

She did, however, lose interest when she heard that one of her pigeons who had decided not to pay off on his bet mysteriously fell from one of the upper floors of a local hotel.

She headed for Hollywood and the start of her movie career.

In the end, making movies was tougher than hustling saps in Vegas or hitting trick shots for the locals. But at the very least, it was safer for a woman who became close to Elvis, Marilyn, Sinatra, and the Rat Pack—and a lot more interesting.

ANDREW CARNEGIE

One afternoon in 1901, Andrew Carnegie was playing golf with J. P. Morgan. The two had been discussing the sale of Carnegie's corporation for some time, and in mid-round they finally agreed on a price of $250 million.

This, naturally, is often cited as irrefutable proof that the business of American business is golf.

At about this time, Carnegie—a passionate if mediocre golfer—somehow managed to make a hole in one. A few days later a friend—who had read about the deal with Morgan— came up and roundly congratulated Carnegie.

"Thank you," Carnegie said. "It's my first hole in one, but how did you hear about it?"

BILLY CASPER

A lot of people believe Billy Casper might be the most underrated great player in history. They've got a pretty good case.

Casper won fifty-one tournaments on the PGA Tour, including two U.S. Opens and a Masters. His win in the 1966 U.S. Open at the Olympic Club, when he caught Arnold Palmer on the last nine on Sunday and then beat him in a playoff, is one of the great comebacks in golf. For his part, Casper believes a trip to Vietnam helped him beat Palmer.

"The soldiers reminded me of lions," Casper recalled. "They'd lie around in the sun, resting and storing up their energy, until it was time to act. Then they'd seize their opportunities and make the most of them. On that last day in the Open, I really didn't think I had a chance to win. I was five strokes back going into the last nine. But then Arnold began hooking the ball badly, and for the first time I could see he was panicking. I had never seen him do that before. I thought about those soldiers and said, This is my opportunity—it's time to move in for the kill. I just tried to put pressure on him, and it worked. I caught him on Sunday, and then I caught him again in Monday's playoff. A lot of his friends think he's never been the same competitor since that Open. They might be right. I know I wasn't."

In the months leading up to the 1998 U.S. Open at the Olympic Club, writers doing preview pieces sought out both Casper and Palmer for their thoughts on the 1966 Open. Naturally, Casper was happy to talk about his win. Palmer wasn't quite as thrilled.

"I ran into Arnold at a tournament, and he said, 'You know, I'm getting a little tired of talking about that Open,'" Casper recalled on the eve of the '98 Open. "I told him he shouldn't mind. It kept his name in the papers."

As if Arnold Palmer ever had to worry about getting his name in the papers.

CHURCH AND STATE

Boston is arguably the most Irish community in America, and the influence of the Catholic church runs wide and deep in the city.

One day, during the 1988 U.S. Open at The Country Club in Brookline, a writer was having lunch after a round of golf at one of the nearby clubs. As the weekend was approaching, he asked the waiter where the nearest church was.

"A Catholic church?" the waiter asked.

"No, Episcopal," the writer said.

"Oh, junior varsity Catholic," the waiter replied.

HENRY COTTON

Henry Cotton, who won three British Opens in the years around World War II, was one of the greatest golfers England ever produced. But if it wasn't for a particularly brutish headmaster at the London school he attended as a boy, he might never have taken up the game.

"Well, you see, cricket was really Henry's first great love," remembered the late Peter Dobereiner, the talented and prolific writer who was a close friend of Cotton's. "Even as a boy, Henry was unusually headstrong. One day he got into an argument with his headmaster, who threatened him with that old public school favorite—caning. Henry wouldn't hear of it, and the headmaster told him he would not be allowed to play cricket again for his school. Henry simply told him that was fine and that he'd take up golf, which he did with considerable passion."

And success, as well.

BEN CRENSHAW

Even as a kid, when he was first learning the game, Ben Crenshaw was interested in golf course design. As he grew older, this was coupled with his passion for the game's history. The two came together in 1968, when he played in the U.S. Junior Amateur at The Country Club in Brookline, Massachusetts. It was the young Texan's first exposure to the classic courses of the Northeast, and he was hooked.

"It was my first trip east, and I remember it as though it was yesterday," said Crenshaw. "It was my first time on a true championship course. It was my first time playing in a formal competition at a proper club, and it was my first USGA competition. But one thing that stands out in my memory is that members hosted a barbecue for us and, despite the heat, the men all wore coats and ties. That was a big difference from barbecues we had back home in Austin."

As a student at the University of Texas, Ben Crenshaw won three NCAA championships and was widely considered the best amateur in the country. He was certainly the most

sought-after player by the directors of the big amateur tournaments. In fact, he received so many tournament invitations that both his father and his college coach screened them.

In the early '70s, the Northeast Amateur was attracting many of the top amateurs, but the player tournament director Bob Kosten really wanted was Crenshaw. He knew Crenshaw could really put his tournament on the map, and if it took a trip to Texas to get him, so be it.

Kosten flew to Austin and finally caught up with Crenshaw on the golf course. He told Crenshaw what a great tournament the Northeast Amateur was.

Ben was polite but noncommittal.

Kosten told him about all the great players who had won the Northeast Amateur and how strong that year's field was.

Ben was polite but noncommittal.

Kosten told him how beautiful suburban Providence, Rhode Island, was in the summer.

Ben was still polite but noncommittal.

Then Kosten mentioned that the tournament was played at Wannamoisett Country Club, a beautiful Donald Ross design that many people considered one of the master's finest works.

That was all it took. Crenshaw came north that summer and won, and the tournament became one of his favorite events. The Northeast Amateur was finally on the map, big-time.

♀

JIMMY DEMARET

Jimmy Demaret and Gene Sarazen were cohosts of the old "Shell's Wonderful World of Golf" series that ran in the 1960s and early '70s. Demaret's quick wit was one reason for the show's success.

During one match, Demaret and Sarazen were interviewing Billy Casper's wife, Shirley. In answering a question, she became momentarily confused and called Demaret "Gene."

"You think I look like Gene?" said the younger Demaret. "We better get the makeup guy over here in a hurry."

"Jimmy Demaret was a great friend of Bob Hope's," recalled Dwayne Netland, a former senior editor at *Golf Digest* who coauthored a bestselling golf book with Hope. "Bob had almost a professional admiration for Demaret's sense of humor. One time they were playing in the Crosby. Bob hooked his tee shot on the first hole out-of-bounds. Demaret looked at him and said, 'That's okay, Bob, there's always next year.' Bob loved it."

Another year at the Crosby, Demaret was on the tee when Phil Harris, nursing a world-class hangover, whiffed not once but twice.

"Don't choke now, Phil," Demaret said. "You've got a no-hitter going."

GARDNER DICKINSON

Gardner Dickinson, who died in 1998, was something of a rarity. He was an outstanding player who was also a skillful and enthusiastic teaching professional. Ben Hogan, whom Dickinson greatly admired, had his own ideas why Dickinson was able to excel at both teaching and playing.

Not surprisingly, Hogan credited Dickinson's willingness to work hard on his game—"to dig it out of the dirt"—for his success on tour. His thoughts on Dickinson's teaching were a little more complicated.

"Gardner enjoyed teaching because he took a great deal of pleasure in helping other people improve," Hogan said. "But he also believed that you could learn as much from studying a bad golf swing as you could from a good swing."

It should be noted here that Hogan wasn't all that sure he agreed with Dickinson on that—and never spent much time trying to find out if it might be true.

Dickinson won seven times on the Tour, on great courses like Doral and Colonial, and beat Jack Nicklaus in a playoff for his final win, the 1971 Atlanta Classic. He had a 9–1 record in Ryder Cup play—the best percentage in the history of the competition—and with a record of 5–0, he and Arnold Palmer were the most successful American team in the competition's history.

But for all his success, his failure to win more tournaments bothered Dickinson. One Sunday night, after another disappointing final round, he sat around drinking scotch with Palmer. As the evening wore on, he finally asked Palmer what was lacking in his game. What was the missing piece?

Palmer thought for a moment. His answer spoke volumes about his own success—and the mind-set of a champion.

"I win because I love to win, but I'm not afraid to lose," Palmer said. "You need to win. That's a big difference. You put too much pressure on yourself."

DISASTERS

After two rounds in the 1991 British Open at Royal Birkdale, Richard Boxall was in excellent position to challenge for the championship. After opening with a 71, he shot a second-round 69 that left him three strokes out of the lead. But when Boxall, then thirty, woke up Saturday morning his left shin ached.

The pain continued as he warmed up prior to his round and steadily worsened as he played the front nine. Still, he was only one over par through the first eight holes and was three strokes off the lead as he stood on the 9th tee.

Then disaster struck.

As he hit his drive, there was a loud crack as his left leg shattered. As the gallery, his wife, and his playing partner, Colin Montgomerie, looked on in horror, Boxall collapsed in horrible pain from the stress fracture and was rushed to a nearby hospital.

The fracture required him to wear a cast for almost five months, and it would be six months before he could take even his first, tentative swings. At least now, though, he can laugh about the whole business.

"I went out in 34 and came back in an ambulance," he jokes.

Playing in the 1953 Bing Crosby National Pro-Am, Porky Oliver came to the 16th hole at Cypress Point in contention for the lead. The 16th, a 222-yard par 3 almost totally across water, is one of the most beautiful and photogenic holes in golf. Sadly for Porky Oliver, it is also one of the most treacherous, particularly when the winds blow in off the Pacific.

On this particular day, the winds were gusting up to forty miles per hour, and Oliver put five balls into the inlet before he finally found dry land. Unfortunately, this particular bit of earth was covered with ice plant, leaving him an all-but-unplayable lie. By the time he was finished, he had taken a 16 and shot himself out of the tournament.

When he finally returned to the clubhouse, there was a message waiting for him.

"Dear Mr. Oliver," the note read. "Please call long-distance operator number 16 regarding your flight home."

Mr. Oliver was not amused.

One of the greatest amateurs America ever produced, E. Harvie Ward won the 1955 and '56 U.S. Amateurs, the 1952 British Amateur, the 1954 Canadian Amateur, the 1949 NCAA as a student at North Carolina, and the 1948 North and South Amateur.

As if all that wasn't enough, he was undefeated as a member of three Walker Cup teams. He was so devastating in match play that the respected golf writer and historian Herbert Warren Wind once named his all-time Walker Cup team and chose Ward as the player he'd want in the most crucial pairing: the last.

"He's the world's greatest amateur, and he represents all the best that there is in golf," said USGA president Ike Grainger after the twenty-nine-year-old Ward won the 1955 U.S. Amateur.

After college Ward moved to San Francisco, and his duels with Ken Venturi are the stuff of legend. People still talk about them today. Perhaps it was his experience, dueling with Venturi at the Olympic Club's venerable Lake Course, that gave him the knowledge and confidence he needed to lead in the 1955 U.S. Open after three rounds.

But disaster struck in the final round.

Ward, playing the 137-yard, par-3 8th hole, hit his tee shot into an old, gnarled tree that guarded the green. The ball stayed in the tree, and Ward's hopes of winning the Open stayed with it. He wound up finishing 7th—the low amateur—as Jack Fleck beat Ben Hogan in a playoff.

If Ward can take any small comfort from his tree problems, it is that he wasn't alone. Many years later, when the tree was cut down, over a hundred balls were retrieved from its branches.

Mark McCumber won The Players Championship in 1988. It was the biggest and most emotional win of the Jacksonville native's career, and for almost three full rounds in 1989, it looked as if he might successfully defend his title.

McCumber came to the nasty, par-3 17th at 9 under par and in the thick of the battle. He hit the island green, which is usually half the battle. He gave his birdie putt a chance but watched it slide just past the hole. Still, he had a cinch par.

Whoops.

McCumber missed the par putt and then, incredibly, missed the half-inch tap-in for bogey.

It would make a nice story to say that McCumber recovered from the shock, but it wasn't to be. He shot a final-round 74 that left him in a tie for fourth, three strokes behind Tom Kite.

JIMMY DURANTE

Jimmy Durante played golf once—and that was one time too many. It wasn't just that he didn't break 100. He didn't even break 100 for the front nine. When the death march finally ended, he asked his caddie what he should give him.

"Why not do us both a favor?" the caddie said. "Give me your clubs."

DWIGHT D. EISENHOWER

President Dwight D. Eisenhower was perhaps the most passionate golfer ever to serve as president and certainly one of the most influential figures in the growth of golf in the 1950s and early '60s.

As president, he was used to a certain deferential treatment from people, and most of the time that extended to the golf course. Mulligans were a given. And so were most short putts. The thought that somebody would play through the President's foursome—uninvited—was all but unthinkable. But it did happen, at least on one bizarre occasion.

One afternoon President Eisenhower and some friends were playing at Augusta National. As they were putting on the 5th green, a ball bounded in front of the green and ran up toward the hole. A few minutes later a man walked briskly onto the green, announced he was playing through, putted out, and left without saying another word—of either thanks or apology.

The man was Ty Cobb.

DAVID FEHERTY

CBS golf commentator David Feherty grew up in Northern Ireland, so you can imagine what went through his mind when he first came face-to-face with American political correctness. For that matter, imagine what sensitivity training classes are like for an Irishman with Feherty's particular genius at seeing the world through his own unique prism.

In 1997, when the PGA Championship was being played at Winged Foot, the management of CBS Sports decided that their golf and football crews should take a day out of their busy schedules to become sensitized to the realities of American life in the closing days of the century. So, in the early hours of the morning the golf announcers piled into limousines for the drive to New York City and their appointment with sensitivity. Feherty, being utterly logical, brought a pillow with him so he could sleep during the forty-five-minute drive.

Everything went fine early in the session, until the woman in charge spotted Feherty sitting comfortably in his chair—cradling his pillow. Naturally, being the sensitive type, she assumed Feherty was taking the whole matter altogether too lightly and took offense. Why did he bring a pillow to class, she asked.

Feherty demurred.

She persisted.

Again, Feherty apologized and insisted that he meant no offense and was looking forward to every single minute of the session.

She wasn't buying it and demanded to know why Feherty was insulting her by bringing a pillow to her session.

With his tongue planted firmly in his cheek, he delivered the coup de grâce.

"Hemorrhoids," he said with a perfectly straight face.

The sensitivity training proceeded apace.

Feherty had another run-in with America's politically correct in 1997. This time he managed to offend animal-rights activists.

During a CBS telecast, play was delayed when a gaggle of geese took their time wandering across a green.

"It's funny how you never seem to have a shotgun when you really need one," Feherty said.

The activists were not amused. Feherty apologized—after a fashion.

"I assure you I've never shot anything but par," he said. "And I haven't done that very often lately."

FOREIGN AFFAIRS

South Africa has produced any number of outstanding players, from Bobby Locke and Gary Player to David Frost and Ernie Els.

Simon Hobday and John Bland are two South Africans who were relatively unknown to Americans until they came over and played well on the Senior PGA Tour. They are long-time friends but are complete opposites.

"What's the difference between a coconut and John Bland?" Hobday once asked a writer. "You can at least get a drink out of a coconut. Christ, I've spilled more bloody beer than he's ever drunk."

Hobday is a brilliant ball-striker, but he'll be the first to admit that he's an awful putter.

"I came to hate putting," Hobday once said. "My feet would actually begin to hurt when I got on a green. It was like I was walking on bloody coals. It got so bad I'd wait off the green until it was my turn to putt, then I'd race to my ball and get it over with as fast as I could."

In France, golfers have a term for a ball that comes to rest on the edge of the cup. It's called a "Danielow," after one Monsignor Danielow.

It seems the good Monsignor, who apparently had a rather broad interpretation of his vow of celibacy, died of a heart attack in the arms—and in the bed—of his young and beautiful mistress.

In certain circles, Monsignor Danielow is still regarded with an awe bordering on reverence—as befits a man of the cloth.

DAVID GRAHAM

By any standard, David Graham's life has been a remarkable success story. He won eight times on the PGA Tour. The highlights include the 1979 PGA Championship, when he beat Ben Crenshaw in a playoff at Oakland Hills, and the 1981 U.S. Open at Merion, when he shot one of the greatest final rounds in Open history. On top of all this, he's a respected designer of both golf clubs and courses.

David Graham's career has been a triumph of determination—even stubbornness—over considerable odds.

He began playing golf as a twelve-year-old lefty in Australia and fell in love with the game, quickly winning junior tournaments. At age thirteen, a local professional convinced him to switch to right-handed clubs. Graham did, but he played horribly and wanted to switch back. Nevertheless, he stuck with the change, and soon his game came around and he was winning again.

At age fourteen he made a fateful decision. He told his parents he wanted to quit school and become an apprentice professional. His mother approved, knowing how much he loved the game, but his father forbade it. He warned David that if he did, he'd be thrown out of the house. When he decided to go ahead, it literally split the family. David and his mother

moved to the rear portion of the house. His father and sister lived in the front. Eventually, his parents divorced.

Some ten years later, David Graham was on the practice range at the 1970 U.S. Open at Hazeltine when a marshal told him there was a spectator who wanted to meet him.

"Hello, David, I'm your father," the man said when Graham approached.

The two went to the clubhouse and ate lunch. The conversation was difficult, as his father tried to explain and apologize for all that had happened between them. In the end, it was too much for David Graham.

"If this is all you have to say, then I don't have time to talk with you," Graham told his father. "I have to go play a practice round. I don't have time during a U.S. Open to talk about all this, when I haven't seen or heard from you in all these years."

With that, Graham went out and tried to finally put the past behind him.

WALTER HAGEN

Walter Hagen loved to travel and was a goodwill ambassador for the United States as he barnstormed his way around the world. That is, at least, most of the time.

On one trip to Japan, the United States ambassador arranged for Hagen to play golf with a person of royal lineage who was, by all accounts, quite mad about golf in general and Walter Hagen in particular.

The appointed hour came—and passed. The embarrassed ambassador assured the prince that Hagen would indeed be right along. And he was, in about an hour or so.

The match went off swimmingly. The prince had a wonderful time. When it was over, the ambassador lectured Hagen on the importance of being on time, especially when it comes to royalty.

"Why, he didn't have anyplace else to go, did he?" Hagen said. "It's not like he had to go back to work and punch a time clock."

Being Mrs. Walter Hagen could not have been easy. He was hardly ever around, and as they say, even when he was around, he wasn't.

One night, he returned home late after another taxing day of being Walter Hagen. As he undressed for bed, his wife mentioned that he wasn't wearing the undershorts he'd put on that morning.

"Jesus Christ!" he exclaimed. "I've been robbed."

"Walter got me good one time when I was a young player," remembers Sam Snead. "We were playing this long par 3 and I wasn't sure what club to hit. I looked over at Hagen, and he pulled his 4-wood out of the bag. I figured the hole must be playing longer than I thought, so I took out a 2-iron. That ball was still rising when it went over the green. Hagen just kind of smiled, put the wood back in the bag, and hit his 4-iron pin high. It taught me to think twice before I tried to go to school on somebody else's club selection."

CLAUDE HARMON

Claude Harmon's win in the 1948 Masters (after not playing in a tournament for six months) is proof enough that he was an outstanding player, but if further evidence is needed, consider some of the rounds he played on some of America's most formidable courses. While he was the professional at Winged Foot, he once broke 70 for fifty-six straight rounds on both the East and West Courses. He also shot 61s on both courses, as well as on neighboring Quaker Ridge, another outstanding A. W. Tillinghast design. Harmon was also the professional at Seminole, the Donald Ross masterpiece in Florida, where he once shot an almost unbelievable 60—a remarkable feat he made sure wasn't lost on his son Dick, a professional and a fine player in his own right.

"When you take your sixtieth stroke, walk in," Harmon said to his son, as Dick headed out to play Seminole. "And let me know what hole you come in from."

None of Harmon's four sons was spared their father's considerable wit or his ability to deliver the needle.

At the 1980 PGA Championship at Oak Hill, Harmon's son Craig, the host pro, qualified for the championship but shot an opening-round 89.

"You cost me money," Claude said. "I bet everyone you wouldn't break 90."

His son Butch played the Tour for a while, without a great deal of success. One day he called to tell his father he'd missed the cut.

"Oh, I must have had today's paper upside down," Claude said. "I thought you were leading the tournament."

Billy Harmon caddied on the Tour for many years, most of the time for Jay Haas. One year at the Masters he was talking with his father and noticed that some food had spilled on Harmon's Green Jacket. Billy began to clean it, when his father cut him off.

"You take care of that white tuxedo of yours [his caddie uniform]," Claude said. "I'll take care of my Green Jacket."

Claude Harmon and Ben Hogan were close friends and played a lot of golf together, especially at Seminole, which was Hogan's favorite course. Hogan would come to Seminole to prepare for the Masters, and he and Harmon had a regular game.

"Claude and Ben would go out, and their regular bet was $10 if you missed a fairway and $10 if you missed a green," explained the late Dave Marr, who was Harmon's assistant at both Seminole and Winged Foot. "That was a perfect game for Ben, but Claude won money as often as he paid it out."

Even when they became successful professionals in their own right, Claude Harmon's sons sought and respected their father's opinions on the game.

One day, Butch and Dick Harmon were discussing sports psychologists and what an impact they could have on improving a player's confidence. Claude listened patiently, at least for a while, but like most pros of his generation, he strongly believed that the best players were self-made. In fact, he had a pretty good example in mind.

"Whatever happened to a square clubface?" he asked. "That's what Hogan used to work on. He'd practice keeping the clubface square through the hitting area. You know, watching those balls fly long and straight down the fairway gave Ben all the confidence he needed."

Claude Harmon was the longtime professional at Winged Foot, and there was speculation that when he retired, one of his sons would succeed him. This presented a problem for the committee charged with hiring a new professional at Oak Hill. They liked everything about Craig Harmon and felt he was the perfect guy for the job. But they worried that the Winged Foot connection might prove to be too strong, and that given the chance, Craig would opt to succeed his father.

"Gentlemen, Oak Hill will be my Winged Foot," Craig Harmon said, and he was right. He's been there since 1972.

BEN HOGAN

At the peak of his career, people began to consider Ben Hogan as some sort of machine who hit every fairway and every green, and who won every time he teed it up. Of course, no one knew better than Hogan just how human he was.

In 1956, the U.S. Open came to Oak Hill Country Club, where Hogan was trying to become the first player to win five U.S. Open championships. For much of the tournament it looked as though he might do it. He was just one stroke out of the lead after the first thirty-six holes, and when Dr. Cary Middlecoff posted two 70s on thirty-six-hole Saturday, Hogan needed to finish 4-4 to force a playoff.

As a huge gallery looked on, Hogan had a thirty-inch putt for a four on 17. The gallery gasped in amazement—even horror—when he missed it. He made a strong bid for a three on 18 but had to settle for a four and a tie for second place.

A lot of people believe Hogan's game never recovered from that missed putt.

He proved to be all too human after all.

Ben Hogan was a legendary competitor, and he was also known as a consummate gentleman. In fact, he took great pride in the way he handled himself and could be a stern critic of players who didn't behave as he felt golfers should.

In his playoff with Jack Fleck in the 1955 U.S. Open at the Olympic Club, Fleck was clearly—and understandably—nervous. On one of the opening holes, Fleck hit two poor shots and told Hogan—who had a putt for a birdie—he'd mark and get out of his way.

"Take your time, Jack," Hogan said. "We've got all the time in the world."

In 1967, Dave Stockton opened the Colonial National Invitation with a 65 that broke Ben Hogan's tournament record and gave him the first-round lead. When he followed it with a 66, he took a ten-stroke lead that seemed insurmountable.

"I walked into the clubhouse feeling pretty good about myself and saw Ben Hogan," Stockton recalls. "I kind of thought he'd say something to me, but he never even acknowledged we were in the locker room together. To tell you the truth, it kind of bothered me."

Stockton went out the next day and skied to an 81 that put him into a tie with Tom Weiskopf. Dejected, he sat in front of his locker and tried to figure out what went wrong. As he sat there, he heard Hogan ask an attendant where Stockton's locker was. Moments later, Hogan came around the corner.

"'I know you expected me to congratulate you yesterday, but I didn't think it would mean that much to you because everyone else was congratulating you,'" Stockton quoted Hogan years later. "'You played two fine rounds of golf and you got your bad round out of the way today. Don't get down on yourself. You can still win this tournament.'"

Sure enough, Stockton went out and edged Charles Coody by two strokes for his first PGA Tour victory.

⛳

Ben Hogan's association with Colonial Country Club stemmed in no small part from his long friendship with the late Marvin Leonard.

Leonard was a successful Fort Worth businessman who made his fortune in department stores and in oil. The two met when the young Hogan was working as a caddie, and from that time on, Leonard supported and encouraged Hogan's interest in golf.

When Hogan first tried his hand on the Tour, he struggled and, by his own admission, went broke at least three times. But Leonard never lost faith in Hogan and, when things got rough, always came through with some money to help the Hogans out.

At one point in the late 1930s, the Hogans were driving to California for the start of the West Coast swing. When Leonard learned that they were down to their last few dollars, he sent them $200. When Hogan finally won some money, he contacted Leonard and tried to repay him.

"Ben, it's enough for me just to know that you want to pay me back," Leonard said. "I don't need your money, but I treasure your friendship."

⛳

"Ben Hogan was a remarkable athlete, which is often overlooked because people just assumed he worked so hard to make up for a lack of talent," recalls Paul Runyan, a two-time PGA champion. "He had the most remarkable hand-eye coordination I have ever seen. One time at Greensboro, we had a weather delay and we were all sitting around in the clubhouse. Ben came up with a game to pass the time. We sat in a circle around a table, with a coin in the middle. Everyone laid their hands on the table, equidistant from the coin. When someone off to the side snapped their fingers, we'd try to cover the coin. The winner was the one who reached the coin first, but if you went ahead of the snap you were out of the game. Ben beat us all like a drum. He was just that quick."

Tom Weiskopf, the 1973 British Open champion, greatly admired Ben Hogan and cherished the rounds they played together. After Hogan's death, Weiskopf was asked just how good Hogan really was.

"I could play and sometimes I could really play," Weiskopf answered. "But even at my best, I never really felt like I belonged out there with Ben Hogan. I felt like a caddie when I played with him."

Jules Alexander, the photographer who snapped the remarkable collection of photos that were published in *The Hogan Mystique*, is a student of Ben Hogan and his career.

"When Hogan was practicing, he'd often hit shots with a cigarette between his lips," Alexander recalled. "When we were looking at the photos with Ken Venturi, he made a remarkable observation: Hogan hit three shots in a row without removing the cigarette. With each shot, the ash on the cigarette grew longer but it never fell off. That's how smooth his swing was. It's almost impossible to do that."

According to Jules Alexander, Hogan once offered this description of a perfectly struck shot: "It goes from the ball, up the club's shaft, right to your heart."

Much has been made of the rivalry between Ben Hogan and Sam Snead, and there's no doubt that they were both fiercely competitive. But when Hogan died in 1997, Sam Snead traveled to Fort Worth for the services. When he saw Hogan's widow, Valerie, he approached her and offered his condolences.

"Valerie, Ben's gone now," he told her. "You've lost a husband, and I feel like I've lost a brother."

After Ben Hogan died, his wife, Valerie, looked back on their life together and captured the pure essence of the man:

"I had the great honor of being with Ben in both the best of times and the worst of times, and he never disappointed me. Not once."

BOBBY JONES

Even taking into account his remarkable record, it's hard for people today to appreciate just how dominant Bob Jones really was. But the anecdotal evidence is overwhelming.

"When Bob played in a tournament, the pros playing on the adjacent fairways would stop and watch him," remembers Charlie Yates, the 1938 British Amateur champion, who lived in Atlanta and was a close friend of Jones. "I always thought that was a pretty good compliment for them to pay to an amateur.

"When Bob would play a friendly match with Tommy Armour, he'd give him a stroke a side and spot him a hole at the start of each nine. In other words, when they teed off on the first hole, Armour was already one up. A writer asked Armour why he'd accept strokes from an amateur. 'Because he's that good,' Armour said.

"He had a similar relationship with Paul Runyan. He gave him one-a-side, and Runyan freely admitted that he 'needed every one of them.'"

J ones carried a plus-four handicap, as did Yates and another East Lake member, Tommy Barnes. The three frequently played together—and Jones usually won. After yet another beating by Jones, Barnes walked into the clubhouse and ran into a friend.

"How'd you make out, Tommy?" the man asked.

"Bob beat me pretty good," Barnes said.

"Tommy," the man said. "Your heart belongs to God, but your fanny belongs to Bobby."

⛳

B y all accounts, Jones had a delightful sense of humor. He could, in the proper company, share a bawdy story with the best of them, and his wit was dry and to the point.

One afternoon, he was sitting with friends on the porch of his cottage at Augusta National. One friend reported a conversation with a Scotsman who, while finding many things admirable about America, detested its heavily wooded courses, preferring the barren links of his homeland.

Jones paused for effect and studied the holes that stretched out before him—each framed by beautiful, towering pines.

"I agree," he said. "I don't see any need for trees on a golf course."

⛳

W hile he was universally known as "Bobby," Jones preferred to be called "Bob" by his friends. He felt it was a little demeaning for a grown man to be called "Bobby," and one day he received a letter from a youngster that proved his point.

"Dear Bobby—When I grow up, I want to be a train engineer. Do you know what you want to be when you grow up?"

Bob Jones was very close to his father, whom everyone called "the Colonel." By all accounts they had a wonderful relationship, even though their personalities were quite different.

"The Colonel was the most rambunctious, energetic man I've ever met, while Bob was very quiet and modest," remembers Charlie Yates. "Bob was known to curse every now and again, but the Colonel could say a hundred words and not use the same swearword twice. One time we had an interclub match and the Colonel was going to play with a man who could match him swear for swear. We decided to have a little fun, so we told each man that the other fellow was a preacher and they had to be on their best behavior. Well, everything went along just fine for about the first fourteen or so holes. But on 15, the Colonel hit a horrible shot and couldn't contain himself any longer.

" 'Goddamn, son of a bitch,' the Colonel yelled, then immediately apologized. 'I'm sorry, preacher. That just slipped out.'

" 'Preacher?' the man said. 'I'm not a preacher. They told me you were a preacher.'

"From that moment on, the sky was blue with profanity," said Yates.

"One time the Colonel was playing the 9th hole at East Lake," Barnes recalls affectionately. "He hit this big slice that went from one side of the fairway into the woods on the other side.

"'Go ahead and get lost in there, you sight-seeing son of a bitch,' the Colonel said."

When Bobby Jones arrived at Merion for the 1930 U.S. Amateur, he had a chance to do what no man had done before or since—close out his celebrated Grand Slam by winning both the U.S. and British Opens as well as the Amateurs in the same year.

He also had a problem. He was such a pure ball-striker that his woods had dime-size dents where he repeatedly hit the ball. The dents had become so pronounced that they were affecting the flight of his shots. But the eve of the National Amateur was no time to be fooling with any new clubs.

As luck would have it, the celebrated professional and club-maker George Sayers was at Merion at the time. Sayers offered to place small metal inserts into the dents. They wouldn't be heavy enough to affect the weight or feel of the clubs, but they should get Jones through the Amateur. Jones, who greatly admired Sayers and his work, took the risk and told him to go ahead.

The inserts worked like a charm. Jones was magnificent all week, won the title, and retired from tournament competition.

Often overlooked in discussions about Jones and the Grand Slam was that the odds of his winning all four national championships were greatly lessened by the fact that he played in the British Amateur only once every four years.

The reason? Jones was not a wealthy man, at least in the years when he was playing championship golf. The only way he felt he could afford to travel to the British Amateur was when the biennial Walker Cup matches were played in the British Isles and the USGA would pay for the team's travel.

In all, Jones played in just three British Amateurs. He lost in the fourth round in 1921 at Royal Liverpool; he lost in the sixth round in 1926 at Muirfield; and he won in 1930 at St. Andrews, beating the 1923 champion Roger Wethered, 7 & 6.

The pressure of tournament competition always weighed heavily on Jones, so much so that he would regularly lose more than ten pounds during the course of a championship.

But as his remarkable career evolved, many people—especially his friends—began to view him as some sort of Superman. When he learned that some close friends were betting large sums of money on him, it only added to the pressure. Years later, he admitted that this was just one more reason why he decided to retire from championship play at such an early age.

Bob Jones played his last round of golf in 1948 at East Lake. One of his playing partners was Tommy Barnes, a fine amateur.

"We started on the back nine," Barnes remembers. "We came to the 8th hole—our 17th—and Bob was two-under. Bob hit a smothered hook. It was the worst drive I'd ever seen him hit. He made a double bogey and finished the round at even par. He didn't make any excuses, but he said later that he'd been having back and neck pains and some numbness. He felt like he was just losing strength. At the time, no one thought that we'd seen Bob's last round. No one could have imagined what the future held for Bob. Not in their worst nightmares."

Jones went to the hospital, where three growths were discovered on his cervical vertebrae. Two operations did nothing to ease the pain. Finally, in 1955, at age fifty-three, he was diagnosed with syringomyelia, a rare disease of the nervous system, which gradually wasted his body and resulted in his death twenty-two years later. News of his illness devastated his friends, as did the degeneration of his body over time.

Jones was reluctant to discuss the state of his health, and his friends rarely asked him directly, being acutely aware of how closely he'd always guarded his privacy, even at the height of his fame. But on one occasion a friend asked just what the extent of the disease truly was.

"There are two types of this disease, ascending and descending," Jones explained patiently. "In my case, the paralysis is from my waist down, so I still have my heart, lungs, and so-called brain."

For all his considerable success, Jones's modesty was reflected in his law office in Atlanta. It was smallish, and there wasn't any evidence of his remarkable accomplishments. In fact, there was scarcely any evidence of his great love for the game.

"Bob had a line drawing of the Old Course on one wall," recalls Charlie Yates. "There was another drawing, with Grantland Rice's wonderful reflection on athletic success—and life—that I thought summed up Bob's feelings so beautifully:

> "For when the one Great Scorer comes,
> To write against your name;
> He writes not that you won or lost,
> But how you played the game."

ERNEST JONES

Ernest Jones was a fine player and a widely respected teacher in England in the years prior to World War I. When England entered the war, Jones enlisted in the army. He was badly wounded, and surgeons were forced to amputate one of his legs just below the knee.

Jones spent four months in the hospital recuperating from his wounds. No one expected him to play golf again, but the day after he was discharged, he went out and shot a remarkable 83.

Because of his handicap, Jones became more convinced than ever that the keys to a good golf swing were timing and rhythm. Before long, he could sit in a chair and hit a ball over 200 yards.

To demonstrate his belief in the importance of timing and rhythm, he would tie a penknife to the end of a handkerchief and have his pupils swing it. Invariably, it improved their swings and ball-striking.

THE LONGEST DAY

For most people, a day of golf means a relaxing three to four hours on the course, followed by some time in the grillroom or on the patio, trading stories and lies. But golf at the championship level is a very different story, as one Maurice McCarthy Jr. found out at the 1930 U.S. Amateur at Merion.

On the second day of the thirty-six-hole qualifying round, he came to the 17th hole needing to play the last two holes in two under par or better—no small demand on any course, but especially difficult over the closing holes at Merion. No problem for McCarthy, though. He simply aced the par-3 17th to earn a spot in a playoff for the final match-play spot.

The next morning he teed off in the eighteen-hole playoff, which he won on the 16th hole. He came back to the clubhouse and promptly teed off in his first-round match against Watts Gunn, who had lost to his friend Bob Jones in the finals of the 1925 National Amateur. McCarthy won on the 19th hole. That afternoon he faced the 1926 Amateur champion, George Von Elm. The eighteen-hole match wasn't settled until the 28th hole, when McCarthy finally closed out Von Elm, setting a championship record.

In all, McCarthy played sixty-three holes in one day. His accomplishment was largely overlooked because of something that happened a few days later: Bob Jones beat Gene Homans in the final to complete his Grand Slam and then retired from tournament competition.

NANCY LOPEZ

Leaving aside the fact that Nancy Lopez is one of the greatest women golfers of all time—and one of the most charismatic—the secret to her popularity may lie in her innate graciousness. Like Arnold Palmer, she suffers fools with remarkable patience. Perhaps it all stems back to an experience she had when she was just a kid.

"I was about fourteen, and I went to a men's tournament," she explained one day. "There was a player I idolized, and I really wanted his autograph. I even had one of those little autograph books. I was standing in line waiting for him, and when he finally came along, the person before me asked for his autograph. He told her he didn't have time. I couldn't believe it. I promised right there that if I ever got good enough for people to want my autograph, I'd never refuse to sign, no matter how long it took."

In 1979, Nancy Lopez had a season that put the LPGA on the map. She won nine tournaments that year, including a record five in a row. She was the darling of the press and the galleries, and it was a mutual love affair. She clearly adored the attention, even when it drew the spotlight to her private life.

When her first marriage failed, she took it very hard. A writer friend told her not to worry.

"Look at marriage as a golf tournament," he said. "That marriage was just a practice round."

She thought about it for a moment.

"Okay," she said. "But if I get married again, will that be a pro-am?"

Nancy Lopez got her start in golf by playing with her parents. Her father, Domingo, was her first teacher, and even now, when she has a problem with her game, he can usually solve it—with common sense and without a lot of cosmic theories and psychobabble.

At one point in her career, she was mired in a slump and her frustration was obvious. After one round, she returned to her hotel room and got a phone call from her father.

"Nancy, I know what the problem is," he said. "You're not happy. You can't play this game if you're not a happy person. If you smile, the good scores will return."

Sure enough, he was right. Again.

JOE LOUIS

When his remarkable boxing career ended, heavyweight champion Joe Louis turned his attention to golf. As you might expect, he had enormous power, but his short game left something to be desired. He was a low-handicapper—unfortunately, not as low as he thought. Louis was an easy mark for hustlers, and one who particularly enjoyed playing with him was the notorious Smiley Quick, who was every bit as skilled at plucking pigeons as was the legendary Titanic Thompson.

"It was painful to watch Smiley hustle Joe," remembers Paul Runyan. "He didn't just take his money; he reveled in picking him clean. I've heard that Smiley bought two condominium complexes with the money he took just from Joe alone, and I believe it to be absolutely true."

DAVIS LOVE III

Davis Love's father, Davis Jr., was one of the game's most respected teachers and a fine player as well. He greatly admired Harvey Penick, and people who knew both men were struck by how similar they were, both as teachers and as human beings.

Early on, he recognized young Davis's talent, but he also knew what could happen if that talent wasn't nurtured properly. As important as knowing when to push, Davis knew how hard to push his son.

"If you want to be a great player, I can teach you what you need to know," he told his son as the boy's game was beginning to truly develop. "If you want to just enjoy the game for what it is, I can teach you that, too."

Young Davis didn't hesitate for a second. He told his father that he wanted to be a great player, and together they set off to help him reach his goal. Davis Jr. called it "the Trip" and urged his son to enjoy it.

Several years later, young Davis wasn't making quite as much progress as his father thought he should—and Dear Old Dad didn't think a lack of talent was at the root of the problem. Perhaps, he thought, a little father-to-son psychology was in order.

"Davis, do you remember how you said you wanted to be a great player?" Dad asked. "Well, you're not doing it. I just thought I'd remind you."

Tragically, Davis Love Jr. died in a 1988 plane crash. Ten years later, his son had won thirteen PGA Tour events, including the 1997 PGA Championship.

He had taken his father's lessons to heart.

Coming into the 1997 PGA Championship, Davis Love III had carried the burden as the "best player who hasn't won a major" for an uncomfortably long time. He looked as if he might shed it at the 1996 U.S. Open at Oakland Hills, but bogies on the last two holes kept him out of a playoff with the winner, Steve Jones.

But Winged Foot would be different. Maybe it was because he loved the course. Maybe it was because the PGA Championship had a special meaning for the son of a golf professional whose life was tragically cut short.

Love opened with a 66, then went 71-66 to set the stage for a duel with his friend Justin Leonard, who had won the British Open just a few weeks earlier. The thirty-three-year- old Love began Sunday's round with a two-stroke lead and, by the fourth hole, had stretched his lead to three. After giving a stroke back at number 7, Love's birdie on 8, combined with Leonard's bogey, gave him a four-stroke lead.

But Leonard, who had come from three strokes behind to win the British Open, fought back with birdies on numbers 10 and 12. When Love bogied 12, it looked like shades of Oakland Hills all over again.

As the two played 15, heavy showers began to pound the course. While Love had a comfortable lead coming to 18, his victory was never completely assured until he hit the fairway with a 3-wood then hit a 5-iron approach fifteen feet to the right of the hole.

As he and Leonard approached the green, the rains stopped and a rainbow appeared over the course. The symbolism wasn't lost on anyone. Not Love nor Leonard, Davis's wife and his mother, nor the members of the gallery.

"Look at the rainbow, Davis," people began to yell.

Love couldn't look. He could barely fight back the tears long enough to finish the hole. When he putted out, he finally looked toward the heavens.

The journey, which he had begun as a youngster with his dad, had finally come full circle.

LUCKY BREAKS

In 1966, Jim Ferree finished his final round at a tournament in Akron, Ohio. He was supposed to join a fellow player on a short flight to Chicago, where they were scheduled to play an exhibition. Ferree had played well in Akron, and as he cleaned out his locker, he decided to skip the exhibition and head for the next tour stop.

It was a lucky, even fateful, decision. The plane Ferree was supposed to catch crashed, killing Ferree's friend, 1964 British Open champion Tony Lema.

Jack Fleck, a club pro from Davenport, Iowa, wasn't given much of a chance of winning the 1955 U.S. Open. Even when he made it into a playoff, the odds against him were staggering since he'd be facing Ben Hogan.

The crowds were enormous and the tension ran high as they teed off. Typically, Hogan was polite but didn't have much to say. As they stood on the tee of the 220-yard, par-3 3rd hole, something happened that gave Fleck a glimmer of hope.

"Ben was getting ready to hit when a little rabbit hopped across the green," Fleck remembers. "Ben backed off, and somebody in the gallery wondered if the rabbit was a good-luck charm. We both laughed, then Ben stepped up and hit a 2-iron four feet from the hole. I thought maybe it was Ben's lucky rabbit until I hit. My ball caught the top edge of a bunker, but instead of kicking back, it hopped forward and landed on the green. We both made pars, and as I walked to the next tee, I remember thinking, 'That was my lucky hole.'"

Fleck went on to win the Open by three strokes. The luck had been his after all.

LLOYD MANGRUM

Talk with the players who knew him, and they'll tell you that Lloyd Mangrum, the winner of the 1946 U.S. Open, was a tremendous player who never got the recognition he deserved. The winner of two Purple Hearts for his service as an infantryman in World War II, he was also one tough guy.

"You wouldn't say Lloyd went looking for fights, but he sure didn't look the other way if he saw one coming," Sam Snead recalls. "One time, when he first came out on tour, he was playing a practice round in the group in front of Gene Sarazen. Now, Gene liked to play fast, and he wasn't afraid to hit into the group ahead of him if he thought they were playing too slow. He did this to Lloyd, and finally after about the third time, Lloyd picked up Gene's ball, walked back down the fairway, handed it to him, and told him the next time he'd jam it down his throat. And he would have, too."

⌖

"It is just unbelievable to me how few people realize how good Lloyd Mangrum really was," recalls Byron Nelson. "In the early 1970s I was doing the Westchester tournament for ABC. Susan Marr, Dave's first wife, had a radio program she was doing and asked if I'd come on, which of course I was happy to do. She had a question she'd been asking players all day: 'Who were the seven players at that time who had twenty-one or more Tour wins?' Well, I thought for a minute and named them. I named Lloyd last, and she was amazed. Nobody else knew Lloyd had won that often."

One afternoon, as a favor to a friend, Lloyd Mangrum agreed to go over to Hillcrest Country Club and play a round with George Burns. After they finished playing, they were sitting around having a drink, when Mangrum offered his assessment of Burns's game.

"George," he said. "You're wearing a beautiful cashmere sweater, gorgeous slacks, and a great-looking shirt. You look just like a pro. It's too bad you play like a comedian."

DAVE MARR

Dave Marr died in 1997 after a long and terrible battle with cancer. Although he was suffering and knew that death was near, he never lost his remarkable sense of humor. Shortly before he died, his daughter, Elizabeth, came to visit him in the hospital. Soon, she was overcome with emotion and began to cry.

"Dad, it's so sad," she said.

"Honey, you should see it from my point of view," Marr said.

GARY McCORD

Gary McCord based his successful television career on the shortcomings of his golf game. He happily told anyone who would listen—which included millions of viewers on CBS Sports—that he played the PGA Tour for twenty-five years without ever winning. It worked like a charm, although sometimes people took him a little too seriously.

Playing in the Kemper Open one year, he was hitting balls on the practice tee when he overheard two women talking nearby.

"Look at that," one woman said. "He gets the ball into the air every time."

McCord couldn't help himself.

"Ma'am," he said. "See my name there on the side of my bag? That means I'm a pro. They won't put your name on your bag unless you can get the ball into the air. It's a Tour rule."

H. L. MENCKEN

As one of America's greatest newspapermen and humorists, H. L. Mencken always rose to the top of his game when he found public officials performing at their imbecilic best—or worst, depending on your point of view. One such case was in Baltimore in 1948, when the civic fathers—whom he dismissed as "silly Dogberrys"—decreed that on the city's municipal courses, blacks could play certain days and whites on the others. He referred to this as a "relic of Ku Kluxry."

The following is taken from a column he wrote for the *Baltimore Evening Sun* on November 9, 1948. Mencken was no fan of golf—on either public or private courses—but he instinctively rebelled against those who would make the game a tool of their own bias and stupidity.

Of equal, and maybe even worse, irrationality is the rule regarding golf-playing on the public links, whereby colored players can play only on certain days, and white players only on certain other days. It would be hard to imagine anything more ridiculous. Why should a man of one race, playing (in forma pauperis) at the taxpayers' expense, be permitted to exclude men of another race? Why should beggars be turned into such peculiarly obnoxious choosers?

DR. CARY MIDDLECOFF

For many people playing the game today, Dr. Cary Middle-coff, who died in 1998 at the age of seventy-seven, is an underrated—even unknown—player. That's astonishing. It's also a shame, because he was not only a brilliant golfer but also a splendid raconteur and incisive television analyst for CBS Sports.

Despite being hampered by a bad back that eventually required surgery and forced him off the Tour in 1961, Doc amassed an impressive record.

Doc had a remarkable amateur career. He won the Tennessee State Amateur as a teenager, and as a member of the University of Mississippi golf team, he won one collegiate tournament by twenty-nine strokes. His greatest accomplishment as an amateur, however, came in 1945, when he won the prestigious North and South Open at Pinehurst while paired with Gene Sarazen and Ben Hogan in the final round.

He joined the Tour in 1947 and won the third tournament he played—the Charlotte Open—by tying the course record in the final round. From 1947 until he retired, he won at least one tournament a year. In all, he is credited with thirty-nine Tour victories, including the 1949 and '56 U.S. Opens and the 1955 Masters. He won the 1956 Vardon Trophy for the lowest scoring average and was a member of three Ryder Cup

teams. At the time of his death, only six players had won more Tour events.

🏌

Like his father and two uncles, Middlecoff became a dentist—although he lost whatever limited appeal that profession held for him during a stint in the Army during World War II.

"I was in there for eighteen months, and I filled 12,093 teeth," Doc later recalled. "The Army counted every last one of them. When I got out of the Army, I didn't want to even look at a tooth. All I wanted to do was play golf."

And play he did.

🏌

Cary Middlecoff's father, Herman, was a fine player in his own right and taught his son to play golf at the age of seven. But Doc admitted later that it took a while for him to really take to the game.

"I used to go out and play about nine holes a week with the other kids," Doc said. "By the time I was fifteen or so I was playing fifty-four holes a day, but it wasn't until I was seventeen that I got serious about the game."

Oh.

🏌

Doc's father, Herman, was opposed to his son's decision to try to make a living on tour. In fact, he kept his son's name on the office door for ten years. He also persuaded his friend, Bobby Jones, to try to make young Cary see the error of his ways, to no avail.

In 1955, Doc Middlecoff won the Masters by a then-record seven strokes over Ben Hogan. That was enough for Jones.

"The way Doc filled those seventy-two cavities over the last four days makes me pretty sure I was wrong," Jones said later.

Doc was at once a deliberate and high-strung player. He would worry over his club selection and then meticulously set up over the ball. If he felt even slightly uncomfortable or out of position, he'd back off and start over again.

"I'll admit I was a nervous player," Doc once explained. "Anyone who hasn't been nervous, or choked, is either an idiot or has never been in a position to win a tournament."

"The boys on tour used to kid Doc about being so slow," Sam Snead recalled fondly after Middlecoff's death. "They'd say he didn't give up being a dentist because he wanted to play golf, but because he couldn't find any patients who could keep their mouths open long enough for Doc to get the job done."

Doc Middlecoff was a great front-runner, but his tremendous length also helped him produce torrents of birdies. At the 1957 U.S. Open at the Inverness Club, he closed with two 68s on the final day to make up eight strokes and get into a playoff with Dick Mayer.

Middlecoff, the defending champion, went into the playoff as the clear favorite, but when Mayer arrived on the first tee, a murmur went through the crowd—Mayer carried with him a camp chair, presumably so he could rest while Middlecoff played his shots.

Was it gamesmanship? That's hard to prove, but if it was, it worked. Doc struggled to a 79 and lost by five strokes.

When Doc Middlecoff won the 1956 U.S. Open at Oak Hill, he was so delighted that he gave his caddie $500 from a first prize of $6,000. To put that in some sort of perspective, if 1998 U.S. Open champion Lee Janzen had paid his caddie roughly the same percentage of his prize money, the caddie would have come away almost $39,000 richer.

WALTER MORGAN

Walter Morgan spent twenty years in the U.S. Army—including two tours in Vietnam—and developed into a fine player. After he left the military, he qualified for the Senior PGA Tour, becoming one of the few African-Americans on the Tour. While he has been successful and respected, he's still not as widely known as some of the more prominent players who had come from the regular Tour.

One day he was paired with Jack Nicklaus. The large gallery greeted him with polite applause when he approached his ball on the first tee.

"I'm Tiger Woods," he joked to the crowd, mimicking the Nike commercial.

During a visit to Washington, Walter Morgan visited the Vietnam Veterans Memorial. A man paused and politely asked Morgan why he wasn't reading any of the names of the dead servicemen inscribed in "the Wall."

"I might see the name of someone I know," he said quietly.

MOTHER ENGLAND

In the years before World War I, British Prime Minister Lloyd George divided his time between running the government and playing golf. He often did both from his beloved Walton Heath Golf Club some twenty-five miles south of London. In fact, so many influential members of the government were members at Walton Heath that it was said the Empire was ruled from the Gentlemen's Card Room.

Alas, the fact that Lloyd George lived near Walton Heath and spent so much time there wasn't lost on the country's women suffragettes. One group blew up his house, which earned its leader, Emily Pankhurst, three years in prison. A second group hid in Walton Heath's woods one day when the Prime Minister was out golfing with the boys. When he appeared, they charged out of the woods, knocked him to the ground, and tried to remove his pants.

And people think sexual politics is rough-and-tumble these days.

King James II was Scottish by birth and fiercely proud of his countrymen. One day a couple of English lords challenged him to a game of golf, insisting that, as Englishmen, they were clearly superior players. James scoffed at them, insisting that he could team with a lowly tradesman and beat them.

To prove his point, James enlisted one James Patersone, a humble shoemaker from Edinburgh. Mr. Patersone, as it turned out, was a humble shoemaker only because he spent so much of his time playing golf. He was, in fact, the best golfer in the area.

The Scotsmen neatly handled the Englishmen in their match, and James won a considerable sum of money. To show his gratitude, he built a house for Patersone and had a plaque installed. The plaque was inscribed with a hand holding a golf club and, in Latin, the words "Far and True."

Over the years, golf fashions haven't always stood up to the test of time. For example, check out photographs of any of the Great Britain/Ireland Ryder Cup teams from, say, the 1970s, and you'll get the drift. Of course, some uniforms are better than others. The clothing worn by the Honourable Company of Edinburgh Golfers in the 1700s was splendid, even elegant, and woe to the member who played out of uniform. Take the case of one Lieutenant James Dalrymple.

In 1776, Dalrymple was fined six pints for playing out of uniform. The penalty could have been worse, but he "made a public confession of the heinousness of his crimes."

The 1973 British Open at Troon was played in absolutely horrible weather, even by the soggy standards of the Open championship. The winds howled and the rains were ferocious. The conditions were so bad that a writer in *The Times* of London observed that Saturday was the type of day when "surely whiskey must have been invented."

The weather notwithstanding, 17,000 spectators came out to watch Tom Weiskopf duel Jack Nicklaus and Johnny Miller down the stretch for his greatest victory.

The British people have always been known for their sense of fair play, and that is certainly true at the celebrated Sunningdale Golf Club outside London. The members go so far as to have their own handicap system to ensure fairness.

The Sunningdale Handicap works like this: once a player falls two down in a match, his opponent gives him an additional stroke a hole until the margin is reduced to one-down.

At Royal Blackheath Golf Club, in the southern suburbs of London, the club's rich traditions extend from the golf course to the clubhouse.

For example, jackets and ties are strictly required for gentlemen in the clubhouse, and while the club keeps a few odd spares around for visitors, they tend to be on the mismatched and garish side.

"Perfect for the Yanks," one member sniffed.

Members who violate the club's rules are subject to the traditional fine of a gallon of claret—and high-quality claret, at that. We are not talking twist-off tops here.

The monthly club dinners are elaborate affairs. Haggis, a traditional Scottish dish, is served with single malt Scotch whisky. Then people drink a toast from a quaich, a traditional silver drinking cup that is passed between members as they rise and stand at attention. One member pours a drink for the man next to him. As he drinks, the members on either side face away from him as if they are on guard. On occasion, a double-sided quaich is used. This quaich is made up of a large cup and a small cup. The size of the cup selected is said to reflect how the server feels about the served.

Royal Blackheath also has a peculiar rule that states that all bets must be settled either on the golf course or in the clubhouse. This stems from one postdinner swimming challenge that saw both members—well into their cups—nearly drown in one of the course's ponds.

The British are big on tradition, which is certainly admirable, especially when it comes to golf. Take the British Open, for example.

In 1946, Sam Snead arrived at St. Andrews for the British Open. He had never seen anything like the place, with its huge double greens, seemingly random bunkering, and somewhat unkempt conditions. On top of all that, he had a succession of caddies that could only be termed "colorful."

"I had this one old boy in my first practice round," Sam recalls. "We got to one of the greens, and he pointed to a spot and said that's where the pin would be on the last day. I asked him how he could be so sure. He gave me kind of a funny look and said, 'Because that's where it's been for the last fifty years.' And he was right, too."

BYRON NELSON

Back in the early days of the Masters, the old Bon Air Vanderbilt hotel hosted big pretournament Calcuttas where people would bid—often enormous sums—on individual players or, in some cases, pools of players.

In 1938 Byron Nelson, the defending champion, agreed to appear at the Calcutta as a favor to Masters officials, even though he had very real reservations about gambling. After waving to the crowd, he went to the back of the room to watch the action unfold. Bidding would begin at $100, and if no one bid on a player, he would be pooled with groups of other players.

When Ben Hogan's name was called, the room was silent. Feeling bad that his boyhood friend's feelings might be hurt, Nelson bought Hogan for $100—the only time he ever participated in a Calcutta.

"The next day Ben asked if he could buy half of himself back from me, and of course, I said that would be fine," Nelson remembers. "It took Ben a little time to scrape up the $50, but he finally did. We never made any money, because Ben finished twenty-fifth, but I'd like to think it gave him a little boost of confidence."

Byron Nelson, Ben Hogan, and Sam Snead were all born in the same year and competed against each other hundreds of times. Here's one for the trivia books: how often did they finish 1-2-3?

"The peculiar thing is, as far as I know, it only happened once," Nelson recalls. "It was at Houston in 1946."

And for bonus points, what was the order of finish?

"I won, Ben was second, and Sam was third," says Nelson.

One of Byron's fondest memories is of a match he and Bob Jones had with Gene Sarazen and Henry Picard, the winner of the 1938 Masters, at Augusta National in the early 1940s.

"Bob was past his prime, but he was still a beautiful player," Nelson remembered. "He shot a 31 on the back nine, and I don't think he came close to missing a shot. There was a stretch in there where Gene and Henry made seven straight birdies and never won a hole from us."

It's a tradition at the Masters that the defending champion gets to pick the menu for the annual Champions Dinner on Wednesday night. When it was Tiger Woods's turn, he showed that for all his maturity and success, he was still a kid at heart: he ordered cheeseburgers, chickenburgers, french fries, and milk shakes for the guys.

Naturally—or at least not surprisingly—there was grumbling from some of the past champions. But Byron Nelson wasn't one of them.

"Tiger," Byron said as the meal was served. "I'm sure glad you ordered these cheeseburgers, 'cause Peggy [his wife] won't let me have them at home and I sure do like them."

JACK NICKLAUS

After a brilliant amateur career, Jack Nicklaus turned pro in 1961. His first victory as a professional came at the 1962 U.S. Open at Oakmont, when he beat Arnold Palmer in a playoff. Still, for all his obvious talent, not all his fellow professionals were all that impressed in the beginning.

"Right after Jack won the Open, we went to Portland for the next tournament," remembers 1959 PGA champion Bob Rosburg. "I used to travel a lot with Fred Hawkins, and he said, 'Jack might be good, but I'd like to see how well he'd do if he lived like we do.' It got back to Jack, and he went out with us every night for a few drinks. I guess it didn't bother him too much. He won by four strokes, and that included a two-stroke penalty. After the tournament, I asked Fred what he thought. He said, 'I guess he can play.'"

People will argue forever whether Jack Nicklaus was, in fact, the greatest golfer of all time. But there's no doubt that there's never been a player with a greater sense of sportsmanship. Witness this incident from the 1981 Masters.

Nicklaus was paired with Greg Norman in the first round. Norman was playing in his first Masters and was understandably nervous. That he was paired with the player he admired most in the world didn't help matters, either.

On the first hole, with huge galleries lining both sides of the fairway, Norman pushed his drive down the right side of the hole. As they walked down the fairway, Nicklaus put his arm on Norman's back.

"I don't know about you, but I'm just hoping that by the time we reach the top of the hill, my feet will finally be on the ground," Nicklaus said. "I'm always nervous here. Just take a deep breath, and let's have some fun out here."

E arlier in Norman's career, Nicklaus had shown the Australian another act of kindness.

They were paired together in the Australian Open. Norman was just twenty-one but was already being praised as the next great player to come from Down Under.

After he and Nicklaus were introduced on the first tee, Norman got up and topped his drive. It ran along the ground and came to rest in a tree just thirty yards from the tee, setting the tone for a very long day that would see Norman wind up shooting an 80.

After the round, Nicklaus sat with Norman for a half hour in the locker room, consoling him and urging him to come to America and take a shot at the PGA Tour. Despite the 80, Nicklaus knew Norman had the game to win against the best golfers in the world. He just wanted to make sure Norman knew it, too.

Joe Murdoch, a member of the Philadelphia Cricket Club, is one of the foremost experts on golf collectibles and memorabilia. His own collection of books numbers more than 2,500 volumes, and as one of the founders of the Golf Collectors Society, he is often called upon to appraise estates.

One year he appraised the estate of a wealthy California collector. As a gift, he received an extremely rare, pristine second edition of the famous 1743 Scottish poem "The Gowff." Naturally, Murdoch was very thankful for the generous gift, but he couldn't help but think that it would be a pity—even a tragedy—if the collection was broken up.

Finally, he came up with what seemed to be an excellent solution: he wrote Barbara Nicklaus and suggested she buy it as a gift for her husband. A few days later, he got a note from Jack.

"Dear Joe," it began. "Thanks, but I don't have that kind of money."

Incidentally, Murdoch has read every single one of the books in his collection except the five hundred or so instruction books.

He is a wise man, indeed.

It's hard to say that Jack Nicklaus ever experienced a real slump, but if you look at his record, you'll see that 1968 and 1969 weren't exactly gangbuster times for him. True, he won five times, but none of the wins were in the majors, which is what he built his career around.

But in late 1969 his father, Charlie, fell ill with cancer. Nicklaus was extraordinarily close to his father—he called him his best friend and biggest fan—and when Charlie died in 1970, Nicklaus rededicated himself to winning. In 1970 he won the British Open, and in 1971 he won five times, including the PGA Championship.

One year, when the British Open came to St. Andrews, Jack Nicklaus and Ben Crenshaw decided to try to hit some gutta-percha golf balls with clubs from that era.

Crenshaw hit first and sent the ball some two hundred yards down the fairway—a remarkable accomplishment, all things considered.

When it was Jack's turn, the ball nose-dived and ran along the ground for about fifty yards. The next shot wasn't much better.

"There must be something wrong with that ball," Nicklaus said, shrugging it off.

"Jack has a good sense of humor and can really give you the needle," remembered the late Dave Marr. "Back in 1972, he lost the Tournament of Champions in a playoff to Bobby Mitchell. Bobby took some of his winnings and bought a toupee. About a month later he ran into Jack at a cocktail party. Jack took a look at the hairpiece and said, 'Bobby, I always knew winning was great, but I didn't know it could make your hair grow back.'"

At the 1998 Masters, Jack Nicklaus, then fifty-eight, shot rounds of 73-72-70-68 to finish in a tie for sixth place. After completing play on Sunday, an interviewer congratulated him on his great "accomplishment." His reaction tells a lot about Jack Nicklaus.

"What accomplishment?" Nicklaus asked, a look of disbelief written across his face. "I didn't accomplish anything. I didn't win."

By every account, Jack and Barbara Nicklaus are superb parents. But being the child of a celebrity isn't always easy. So you can imagine Nan Nicklaus's reaction when a couple of girls in her dorm approached her on her first day at the University of Georgia.

"Hey, are you really Jack Nicholson's daughter?" one girl asked. "He was great in *The Shining*."

GREG NORMAN

Once Greg Norman decided to concentrate on golf, he devoted himself to the game with a singular focus and dedication. That he might fail never seemed to occur to him.

One day he told a group of his friends that he had a vision of the future and that the future looked like this: "By the time I'm thirty, I'm going to be the best golfer in the world, I'm going to be married to an American, and I'm going to be a millionaire."

As you might expect, his friends greeted this prediction with more than a little skepticism. A lot more, as a matter of fact. They were positively scornful.

"When I do, I'm going to call each of you," said Norman.

By the time he was thirty, Greg Norman was arguably the best golfer in the world.

He was happily married to an American, the former Laura Andrassy, and deliriously happy as a parent.

He was, at the very least, a millionaire.

And he did call his old pals, just to give them a friendly reminder.

From the time he turned pro in 1976, Greg Norman built his game around the idea that someday he'd be competing in the United States.

To that end, he worked to develop a swing that would allow him to hit the ball high and stop it quickly on the greens. To do this, he would go to a spot near the practice ground at Royal Queensland, where he was laboring as an assistant to professional Charlie Earp, and practice launching 5-irons up over the tree. In typical Norman fashion, he wasn't satisfied until he could move in as close as possible to the tree and still cut the ball up over the highest limbs.

"Greg," said Earp, one of Australia's most respected teaching pros. "It's fine to hit the ball high, but you've got to learn to get it down."

"I've got to hit it high in America," said Norman, rocketing another ball over the tree.

"Yeah," said Earp, "but you'll be playing in England before you'll be playing in the States, and if you hit that shot there, you'll be playing your next shot from Paris."

When Greg Norman won his second professional event, the 1977 Martini Invitational on the European tour, he shot a final-round 66 to beat Simon Hobday by three strokes.

An enterprising writer looked at the scoreboard and noticed that it read 10 66 (a 10-under-par total for the tournament and 66 for his day's round). The writer recalled that in the year 1066, an event of some historic note began: the Norman Conquest.

A thousand headlines were launched that afternoon.

114

Greg Norman's loss to Nick Faldo in the 1996 Masters was one of the most dramatic collapses in the tournament's history. Norman led by seven shots going into the final round, and many—if not most—people figured he was a lock to finally win on a course so perfectly suited to his game.

"Not even you can find a way to screw this one up now, Greg," said his friend, the well-respected British writer Peter Dobereiner.

For once, sadly, Dobereiner was wrong.

Norman began losing strokes early, and Faldo finally caught him on the 11th hole. From there, Faldo was relentless and wound up winning by five strokes. After they putted out on 18, the two men embraced and Faldo admitted he was at a loss for words.

"I don't know what to say," he told Norman. "I just want to give you a hug."

In the odd way it sometimes happens in both sports and life, people looked at Norman with a new respect and admiration for the way he took the loss. He answered all the questions candidly. The letters and telegrams poured in. The ovations that greeted him in the tournaments that followed were both louder and warmer than they had ever been before.

One person who was moved by Norman's actions was a man who knows something about winning—and losing—under pressure.

On a wall at Ted Williams's house, the great Red Sox hitter and outfielder hung photos of just two golfers: Bobby

Jones, for the grace he showed in victory, and Greg Norman, for the courage he displayed in defeat.

Norman's final round that Sunday in 1996 was so devastating and painful that some people literally could not watch as it played out slowly over the afternoon. One of them was Ben Crenshaw, the two-time Masters champion.

Crenshaw was in Butler Cabin, working as an analyst for CBS Sports. At one point, after Norman's last chance died with a tee shot into the water on 16, Crenshaw quietly removed his microphone and walked outside onto a small patio. There, alone with his thoughts and his profound sense of history, he quietly shed a tear for Greg Norman.

Another was Norman's close friend, Nick Price. As Norman's nightmarish afternoon began to play out, Price was watching on television in the locker room at Augusta National. Before long, it became too painful to endure.

"I knew just how much the Masters means to Greg," said Price. "I could see what was happening, not only to his game but to him as a person. I couldn't watch it."

So Price cleaned out his locker and left for the airport.

Greg Norman was playing a practice round in the 1988 U.S. Open at The Country Club in Brookline, Massachusetts. On one hole, he muscled a wedge shot out of the high, thick rough that came to rest on the green, but a long way from the hole.

"That's not such a hard shot," he heard a man say in the gallery.

"Oh yeah?" Norman said. "Why don't you come out and try it."

Sure enough, the man came under the ropes, took Norman's wedge, and knocked it inside Norman's ball. He got a huge ovation from the gallery—and a high five from Norman.

Greg Norman's loss to Larry Mize in the 1986 Masters was one of the most painful in a career marked by soaring triumphs and bitter disappointments. Norman, Mize, and Seve Ballesteros were tied after seventy-two holes. Ballesteros was eliminated after the first playoff hole, the par-4 10th. Both Norman and Mize missed the green on the dangerous 11th.

Mize was away—some 140 feet from the hole—and stunned the golf world by chipping in.

Norman, who figured to have the advantage if they tied the hole and went on to the par-5 13th, looked on in utter disbelief, then missed his own attempt.

After sitting through a press interview that could not have been easy for him, his daughter, Morgan-Leigh, gave him a hug and consoled him the way only a little girl can console her father.

"Daddy," she said, "even though you didn't win, can we still have a party anyway?"

SE RI PAK

In 1998, the LPGA's Se Ri Pak had the kind of rookie season that most people can only dream of.

The twenty-year-old South Korean won four tournaments, three of them in a four-week stretch. As if all that weren't enough, two of the victories were majors—the LPGA Championship and the U.S. Women's Open. She was the first woman to win the Open in sudden death after the end of an eighteen-hole playoff, and she was the youngest player in LPGA history to accomplish all this.

While many players might be envious of her accomplishments, it's a safe bet that not many would like to undergo the training Pak went through as a kid.

Se Ri Pak's father, Joon Chul Pak, was a talented amateur golfer. One day, when he was out practicing, Se Ri, then eleven, asked if she could try to hit a few shots. While she was a good athlete, he was surprised by how quickly she picked up the basics.

119

"In less than thirty minutes she had a perfect grip and was hitting very good shots," her father said.

He had seen the future. Now he would push her toward it.

Despite Se Ri Pak's understandable reluctance to all but give her life over to golf at such an early age, her father would not be moved by her pleas or arguments or even her tears. He drove her relentlessly. They would work in wilting heat or in the winter when ice would form in her hair.

"He made me strong," she said later. "Many times I wanted him to give me a chance to rest or to spend time with my friends. But then I would tell myself to just show him that I could do what he wanted, that I could do anything I wanted. Finally, I got to the point where I wanted to do well because I loved the game and loved my parents and I wanted to prove that my father knew what he was doing. That he wasn't crazy."

For Joon Chul Pak, it wasn't enough that his daughter master the mechanics of the game. He would ensure that she was mentally tough as well. There may have well been madness in his method, but there's little doubt that it worked.

There was a cemetery near their home, and they would routinely pitch a tent amid the graves and spend the night. After a while, he began leaving her alone with her thoughts and fears.

"Don't be afraid," he would console her. "I won't let the ghosts get you."

Many people, including his wife, were more than a little skeptical about at least this part of the grand design. But one evening, when she was sixteen, he got the answer he had been awaiting for all those years.

"I was getting ready to leave her one night, and she said, 'I'm warm here now,' meaning she was finally strong enough to be comfortable," he said. "We never went back to the cemetery."

It didn't take long for Se Ri Pak to become well aware of the bitter realities of golf in South Korea. It was a game for the wealthy and privileged, with membership fees at private clubs running from $200,000 to over $1 million a year. While her parents had sacrificed so she could enjoy the benefits of a membership, there was never any feeling of being part of the country's golf elite. Indeed, the truth was far from it.

In her sophomore year in high school, Se Ri entered a prestigious tournament, the Golf Digest Cup. Her father, spotting a group of parents nearby, went over and tried to strike up a conversation.

What happened next wasn't pretty, to be sure, but without a doubt it left a strong impression on a young girl who worshiped her father.

"The parents completely ignored me," said her father. "They treated me like I wasn't even there, because their social status was so much greater than ours. I called to Se Ri and told her to come over to where the trophy was being displayed. I picked up the trophy and handed it to her.

" 'This is yours,' I said. 'Go ahead and take it.'

"Se Ri took the trophy, and the parents looked at me as though I was a madman," he went on. "This greatly angered me, so I shouted to them, 'So what if I dare touch your trophy. My Se Ri is going to win it anyway.' "

Joon Chul Pak remembers his daughter's smile. He remembers the scorn reflected in the faces of the other parents. And he remembers that his daughter won the tournament and took the trophy home with her.

Her sense of purpose and resolve became so great that, by the time she was in her late teens, her parents would often have to all but beg her to stop practicing.

"If Se Ri hit a bad shot during a round, she would go out and practice it over and over until well after dark," her father recalled. "Many times it would be near midnight and we would call to her to come in. She would beg us for just five more minutes."

While she still struggles with her English, Se Ri Pak was able to succinctly sum up one reason for her remarkable success.

"I have no nervous," she once told 1991 U.S. Women's Open champion Meg Mallon.

And not many other weaknesses, either.

GARY PLAYER

When the young Gary Player arrived at St. Andrews in 1955 for his first British Open, he was understandably nervous and excited.

"I stood on the first tee and hit a screaming hook," Player remembers. "I was paired with this old fellow, and he asked me what my handicap was. I told him I was a professional here to play in the Open championship. He thought for a second, looked at where I had hit my drive, and said, 'Well, you must be a very good chipper and putter.'"

With two holes left to play in the 1974 British Open at Royal Lytham & St. Annes, Gary Player had what seemed to be an insurmountable six-stroke lead over England's Peter Oosterhuis.

But on the par-4 17th, his approach missed the green to the left and wound up in the tall, thick rough. After a frantic search that involved Player, his caddie, Rabbit, Oosterhuis and his caddie, and people from the gallery, Player's ball was finally found—just moments before the five-minute time

limit expired. He made a bogey but still had a comfortable lead coming to the home hole.

After a good drive, he faced a fairly straightforward second shot to an easy pin placement.

"What do you think, Rabbit, can I win?" Player asked his caddie.

"Ray Charles could win from here," Rabbit said.

Whoops. Not so fast, Rabbit.

Player hit a solid shot and then watched with a certain relief as the ball landed short of the pin and started rolling toward the hole.

He looked on with delight as it ran closer to the hole. Surely this was going to make for a triumphant victory march up the 18th fairway. He might even have a tap-in, and what could be better than that?

Then, as he watched in dismay, the ball ran across the green toward the old brick clubhouse. It came to rest not near the clubhouse but virtually against it.

To his great credit, Player didn't panic. He sized up the shot and decided to use his putter and play left-handed, running the ball back to the green. Still, it wouldn't be an easy shot.

"I remember that the gallery was along the side of the clubhouse, and their shadows kept moving across the ball as they jockeyed for position. There was this one old codger who opened one of the windows to get a better view, and of course the members were happily drinking away in the clubhouse as though it was the finals of the club championship."

As he did so often in his career, Player pulled off a remarkable shot. The ball came to rest about twelve feet from the hole, and he two-putted for his third British Open title.

Later, Player and his wife, Vivian, were having dinner when a photographer approached and asked if he might take their picture with the Open trophy. To their horror, they realized that they had left the Old Claret Jug behind at the clubhouse.

"It suddenly occurred to me that I might be the first Open champion to lose the trophy," Player joked later.

Throughout his career, Gary Player has seemingly willed himself to success by assuming the role of the underdog, even if that has meant inventing some reason why he was the underdog when no other reason appeared obvious—at least to anyone but him.

After two rounds at the 1974 British Open at Royal Lytham & St. Annes, he held a five-stroke lead over the field. Anyone else would have been ecstatic, but not Player. For him, this was a calamity of the first order.

"No man can possibly win with such a lead," he told the press. "You don't know whether to continue attacking the course or fall back and protect your lead. You're totally of two minds. No, I'm afraid I'm done for. I won't be able to play a shot tomorrow."

Naturally, facing such enormous odds, he somehow managed to hold on and win by a mere four strokes.

Gary Player was in Augusta for the 1979 Masters when he got a call from the minister at his church back home in Johannesburg. The clergyman was in the United States on a lecture tour and thought it would be a great idea to come to the Masters. He wondered if Player had an extra badge.

As luck would have it, Player had already exhausted his supply, but as an intensely religious man, he wasn't going to take any chances. He gave the minister his own badge.

Bad idea.

As the minister was entering Augusta National, one of the security guards noticed he was wearing badge number 1—the badge reserved for the defending champion. The minister was hustled off to the tournament office, where he tried—without much success—to explain everything to officials.

It wasn't until Player arrived at the course and was brought to the tournament office that everything was resolved. Naturally, Player, ever the optimist, found something positive about the experience.

"I will tell you that it increased my already high regard for Augusta National," he said later. "What magnificent security they have. First rate, just like everything about the Masters."

When Gary Player joined the PGA Tour in 1957, he already idolized Ben Hogan and tried to mold his game in Hogan's image. Imagine his excitement, then, when after his first round with Hogan, the Great Man took him aside in the locker room.

"Gary, you're going to be a very good player," Hogan said. "Do you practice much?"

"All the time," Player said.

"Double it," Hogan said and walked away.

THE PRESS

Many people treat golf as though it's some kind of religion, but religion and golf don't always mix. Just ask Jim McKay, the veteran television journalist and longtime anchor of ABC's golf coverage.

On Good Friday, when he was fourteen years old, he and his cousin, Frank Callahan, decided to play a little golf at a course called Cobb Creek. On their way home, they passed their parish church, and naturally, since McKay is Irish to the depths of his soul, the guilt began to set in. They quietly went inside the church, leaned their golf bags against the rear wall, and slid into an empty pew.

Safely ensconced in the bosom of the church on one of the holiest days of the year, everything seemed in divine order.

That is, until both bags fell over with a shattering crash.

The good nuns have taken rulers to knuckles for less. A lot less, come to think of it.

George Kimball is a sports columnist for the *Boston Herald*. He's a great bear of a man, with curly red hair and a bushy beard to match. He's also something of a throwback to the days when sportswriters were often as well known for their exploits as the players they covered.

According to legend, one night George was in a bar with a friend. The friend excused himself and asked George to "keep an eye on my drink."

Big mistake.

George took him literally, took out his glass eye, and dropped it in the man's drink.

For many years, *Golf Digest* hosted a Senior PGA Tour event in Rhode Island at the Newport Country Club. One of the highlights was the press day, when writers from around New England would take advantage of a chance to play at the club—which hosted the first U.S. Open and U.S. Amateur— for free.

One year, as part of the fun and games, there was a Closest to the Pin contest on one of the par 3s. To make things a little more interesting, a small company that was building hickory-shafted replicas of old clubs agreed to supply clubs for the contest in hopes of getting a little free publicity from the writers.

As luck would have it, George Kimball was in the first group that day. When he came to the hole where the Closest to the Pin contest was being held, he got up and lashed into the ball.

Well, not exactly into the ball. He hit about four inches behind it. The ball barely moved, but the force did shatter the club.

"It must have been a bad shaft," said George, looking at the sorry remains of the club, still in his hands.

In 1979 John Fought won twice as a rookie on the PGA Tour. At the end of the season he was honored in New York as the Rookie of the Year. He arrived in the city the night before, and an editor from *Golf Digest* met him at his hotel and took him out for dinner.

In the course of the evening they wound up at Runyon's, an East Side bar popular with writers and television types. As luck would have it, CBS golf commentator Ben Wright was there with his then-fiancée, Kitty—two of the most sociable people New York had to offer.

Fought didn't drink alcohol, although he didn't mind watching other people toss back a few. Actually, as it turned out, quite a few. Leaving Runyon's, they stepped into the night and tried to hail a cab on Third Avenue.

"I have to tell you, I've never seen people who can drink that much alcohol," Fought said.

"That's all right," the editor said. "I have to tell you they've never seen anyone who can drink that much Coke."

The late Henry Longhurst was a celebrated and widely respected writer and television commentator. He was an Englishman who felt very much at home in the United

States—or anyplace else where golf was played, for that matter.

Longhurst deeply loved the game, but toward the end of his life, he came to bemoan the track that golf was headed down. He detested golf carts and thought caddies should remain an integral part of the game. He was a traditionalist, in the best sense, and felt change should come slowly to the game.

One lovely spring afternoon, he was holding court on the veranda at Augusta National, drinking with friends and railing—in his own way—against the various outrages he thought were being inflicted on golf in the name of progress.

"Alas, it's still a wonderful game after all these years, the best there's ever been," he said. "The proof lies in the fact that whatever they do to it, they can't ruin it."

Clare Briggs was a prominent cartoonist in the 1920s, best known for his series "When a Fellow Needs a Friend." One of his friends was Bobby Jones, whom he met at the 1924 U.S. Open at Oakland Hills.

One evening Briggs, Jones, and a few other kindred spirits were having cocktails in Oakland Hills' elegant clubhouse. The subject turned to Briggs and his artwork, and he happily began to demonstrate his considerable skills—on the clubhouse walls.

Within days, the sketches had been wallpapered over.

Alas, everyone's a critic.

Sweden became a legitimate—if unlikely—golf powerhouse in the 1990s. Men like Jesper Parnevik and Per-Ulrik Johansson emerged as world-class players, but in the women's game the Swedes were even more impressive.

Paced by the likes of Helen Alfredsson, Liselotte Neumann, and Anika Sorenstam, Sweden produced such an awesome collection of players that six of the twelve members of the 1998 Solheim Cup team were Swedish. For good measure, so was the team captain, Pia Nilsson.

Unfortunately—and perhaps not surprisingly—their golf writers haven't kept pace. Oh, they're fine writers, to be sure. It's just that some of the game's subtleties seem to have escaped them.

Take, for example, the case of the writer from the Swedish tabloid *Aftonbladet*.

One can only imagine the correspondent's excitement when he was given a dream assignment—the 1998 Solheim Cup at the Muirfield Village Golf Club in Dublin, Ohio.

And one can only imagine his confusion when his flight landed in Dublin, Ireland, and he asked directions to the course.

Shirley Povich, the legendary sports columnist who wrote for the *Washington Post* for seventy-four years, might well have owed his remarkable career to golf—or, more precisely, caddying.

As a boy growing up in Bar Harbor, Maine, he got a job caddying at a local country club favored by the wealthy summer crowd. One member, Edward B. McLean, took a particular liking to the seventeen-year-old Povich. McLean was the publisher of the *Post*, and he suggested that Povich leave Maine and come to Washington. He offered Povich two jobs. The first was as a caddie on McLean's personal golf course. The pay was $20 a week. The second job was as a copyboy at the *Post* for the princely sum of $12 a week.

Povich, who had never been out of Maine or even been on a train, jumped at the opportunity. His first loop as McLean's caddie proved to be a memorable one.

He caddied for McLean's good friend, President Warren G. Harding.

NICK PRICE

Nick Price was born in South Africa but was raised in Rhodesia. He joined the Rhodesian air force at a time when the nation was rocked by a bloody struggle between the ruling white minority and the emerging black majority.

Now, Nick Price is not a particularly ideological person, but he saw his duty and resolved to do it. Having said that, he's not crazy, either.

During the induction physical, he was asked if he had any medical conditions that would keep him from serving.

"Well, I do have this skin problem," Price said.

"What's the problem with your skin?" he was asked.

"Bullets go through it," Price replied.

DANA QUIGLEY

Dana Quigley is one of those success stories that make the Senior PGA Tour so appealing. A club pro from Massachusetts, he had long been a successful player in tournaments around New England. When he turned fifty, he decided to give the Senior Tour a shot.

He entered the 1997 Northville Long Island Classic and was medalist in the Monday qualifying. He played well all week, and when he beat Jay Sigel in a three-hole playoff, his eyes filled with tears of joy and relief.

But a few minutes after receiving his trophy and $50,000 winner's check, he got a phone call from his brother, Paul, telling him that their father had died that afternoon after a ten-year battle with cancer.

"It went from being one of the greatest days of my life to the worst day of my life," Quigley said. "My dream was to come out on tour and be successful so my parents would be proud of me. I wanted to buy them a house on the water in Florida. I won, but I just didn't win soon enough. God works in strange ways. The day he took my father's life was the same day he gave mine back to me."

ALLAN ROBERTSON

In the mid-1800s, Allan Robertson of St. Andrews was believed to be the best golfer in Scotland and, therefore, the world. At a time when almost all golf was at match play, he was very nearly invincible. Of course, the fact that he was also a premier club and ball maker didn't hurt either.

One evening he was having dinner with a friend, Jamie Condie, a fine player and a member of one of Scotland's best-known golfing families. Condie kidded Robertson that for all his considerable skills, the real secret of his success lay in his equipment. The two men argued back and forth until finally they agreed to settle the debate with a match the following day. The terms were that the winner of a hole would get to take one of his opponent's clubs.

To his dismay, it didn't take long for Robertson to realize that he had been too generous in giving strokes to Condie. By the time they reached the home hole, all that Robertson had left were his two favorite clubs—his driver and putter. After putting out, he was down to his putter.

Bravely—or foolishly—Robertson agreed to play one more hole, this time with just his putter. A few minutes later, that was lost, too.

LAURANCE ROCKEFELLER

In the 1950s, Laurance Rockefeller invested some of his family's considerable fortune in the development of a golf resort in Puerto Rico—Dorado Beach, built some twenty miles outside San Juan over 1,500 acres that had been a coconut and grapefruit plantation. It was designed to be one of the jewels in the crown of upscale resorts known as Rockresorts that are sprinkled across the United States and the Caribbean.

Rockefeller, one of America's foremost conservationists, worked closely with Robert Trent Jones on the design of the course, taking pains to make sure that it was developed in a manner that blended comfortably with the environment.

As it happened, Rockefeller was visiting Dorado Beach just after it opened and was persuaded to attend a cocktail party welcoming the guests. "Persuaded" is the key word here, because Rockefeller—a shy man—detested this sort of thing. At any rate he went and, after a few torturous minutes, extended his hand and introduced himself to one of the guests.

"Hello, I'm Laurance Rockefeller," he said softly.

"Right, and I'm Napoleon Bonaparte," the man replied.

With that, Mr. Laurance Rockefeller was out of there.

CHI CHI RODRIGUEZ

Beyond being one of the best-loved players on the Senior PGA Tour, Chi Chi Rodriguez is easily one of the most superstitious. In fact, he's elevated his collection of quirks, beliefs, and hunches to a veritable art form. There's no one who even comes close.

For starters, during any given round he'll carry a lucky walnut, tees in his lucky colors—whatever those colors are that week—lucky coins, and, last but not least, a rock blessed by the Pope. He always marks his ball with the "head" side up and never uses pennies, and if he has a birdie putt, he'll mark the ball with a quarter. If he sees a coin on the ground, he won't pick it up unless it's lying headside up.

When it comes to clothes, he always tries to wear green on Sunday, because it's the color of money. It's also a good bet that he'll never wear red on Thursdays. And if he has a good round, he'll take the same route back and forth to the course for the rest of the tournament.

In one tournament, Rodriguez was staying in a house that had a palm tree planted outside the front door. When he came home after a poor first round, he noticed the palm tree and, since this is a bad-luck omen in his native Puerto Rico, asked to have it removed. It was, and he shot rounds of 66 and 67 over the next two days.

Given all this, you'd expect that receiving a voodoo doll would positively unnerve him. Not at all.

"I was playing a tournament in Jamaica in late 1986," Rodriguez remembers. "I came back to my room and there was a voodoo doll on my bed. It had nails through each eye and each knee."

Did it work?

Apparently not, since 1987 was his best year on the Tour.

***

Chi Chi Rodriguez is a player who really made the most of his Senior PGA Tour career. He had won eight times on the regular Tour and was a member of the 1973 Ryder Cup team, but when he turned fifty, his career really took off. He has twenty-two wins and has emerged as one of the Tour's premier players. In fact, he's doing so well as a senior that he's come up with a plan to keep the party going.

"I'm going to set up a tour for players eighty and over," he explains. "You play three-hole tournaments, one hole a day. At the end of three days, the guy who can remember what he scored on each hole wins the $1 million first prize."

***

"When I first came out on tour, Bob Goalby gave me a good piece of advice," Chi Chi recalls. "He told me to play my practice rounds with Sam Snead every chance I got. He told me, offer to play for a little money—a $5 nassau. You might lose $20 or so, but you'll get a four-hour playing lesson and it will be the best lesson you'll ever get."

⛳

"Chi Chi came up to me one day and asked me to look at his swing," Sam Snead recalled. "We went out to the practice range, and I watched him hit about three balls. Then I said to him, 'Cheech, remember when you were playing good, you'd kind of fall over after you hit it? Well, now you're falling over when you hit it.'

"He hit a couple more balls and just striped them. He told me if he won he'd give me $5,000. Sure enough, he won the tournament and his caddie came up to me and handed me a check for $5,000. He told me, 'Chi Chi said to thank you—and don't cash the check until next week.'"

⛳

One day early in their marriage, Chi Chi Rodriguez and his wife, Iwalani, were sitting outside a clubhouse when a stunning woman walked by. That Chi Chi watched her every movement didn't go unnoticed by Iwalani—and she let him know about it.

"Now, honey, just remember that when we married I gave you my heart, but not my eyes," he said.

⛳

BOB ROSBURG

Bob Rosburg won seven tournaments on the PGA Tour, including the 1959 PGA Championship, but for many people these days, he's best known as the veteran foot soldier for ABC's golf coverage. His insights and candor make him both a rarity and a delight.

Rossie was literally a child prodigy. Growing up in San Francisco, his father started him playing the game as a two-year-old at Harding Park, the wonderful municipal course. As he improved, his father joined The Olympic Club, where, as a twelve-year-old, Rossie beat the legendary Ty Cobb in the club championship.

The nation, however, had learned about Rossie's skill years earlier. When he was just three or four, he appeared on the Fox-Movietone newsreels, which were shown weekly at movie theaters all over America.

One of the people captivated by Rossie's performance was Admiral Richard Byrd, the polar explorer. Byrd wanted to use Rossie as an opening act to attract people to his films and lectures.

For six weeks, Rossie and his mother toured the country. He'd go on stage and hit balls for a while, then the newsreels would be shown. When they were finished, Byrd would come onstage and give his lectures to packed houses.

THE RULES

The Rules of Golf can be a little complicated, even for experts. Take the case of Tom Meeks, the Director of Rules and Competitions for the United States Golf Association.

In 1978, he was working at the U.S. Junior Amateur. The first match of the championship pitted the defending champion and medalist, Willie Wood, against Mark Brooks, who went on to win the 1996 PGA Championship.

When the time came for the match to start, Wood was among the missing. Meeks thought for a moment and then made his ruling. Brooks would start, and every hole he played until Wood's arrival would count as a win.

Naturally, Brooks took off like a shot and played four holes in about twenty minutes. By that time, Meeks had become concerned about his ruling and called his boss, the highly respected P. J. Boatwright, who at that time was the USGA's Director of Competitions and the game's leading rules expert.

Boatwright was—to put it mildly—incredulous. He told Meeks that in match play, the penalty for missing a starting time was disqualification, unless the player had a good excuse. As luck would have it, Wood had one: a USGA official had given him the wrong starting time. Brooks was brought in off the course, and the match was played. Wood won, 2 & 1.

One afternoon, during a U.S. Junior Amateur qualifier at the Country Club of Fairfield, a rules official was summoned by two players standing near the thick underbrush down the right side of the first fairway.

"Excuse me, sir," one youngster said, very politely. "Could you explain the provisional ball rule to us?"

The official explained the rule.

"Thank you very much, sir," the boy said.

"You're welcome," said the official, and he began to drive off in his cart.

"See, you [blanking, blanking, blank]," the kid said to his playing companion.

In 1998, on the eve of the U.S. Open, the United States Golf Association hinted that it was planning to take action against the ball and club technology that had been developing so rapidly in recent years. Naturally, this created enormous outrage on the part of equipment manufacturers. It also led Rabbi Marc Gellman to muse what life might be like if the USGA had the ability to make rulings on nongolf matters.

Rabbi Gellman, along with his friend Monsignor Tom Hartman, was giving the invocation at the annual Metropolitan Golf Writers dinner in suburban New York. It was a receptive audience for the rabbi's thoughts.

"The USGA doesn't want golf to become too easy, so they want to change the rules," the rabbi said. "If they had their way, the Catholics would have to make hosts smaller, because large hosts might make repentance too easy; Muslims would have their prayer beads checked for grooves that made them too easy to pray with; and Jews would have to reduce the size of dreidels [a child's four-sided, toplike toy], because the big ones are too easy to spin. I think the best thing they could do if they really wanted to make golf a better game is to ban lime-green pants. Now, that would be an improvement."

PAUL RUNYAN

Paul Runyan, who won the 1934 and 1938 PGA Championships, possessed one of the greatest short games in golf history. Small in size and never a long hitter, he made up for what he lacked in power with an uncanny ability to score around the greens. It was a skill that drove longer hitters crazy.

Runyan was so skilled, in fact, that he came out of semiretirement and challenged at the 1953 U.S. Open at Oakland Hills. The winner of twenty-eight Tour events, he was fortyfive years old and a teaching professional. He had even worked for a time selling jewelry. Whatever he was doing to make the mortgage payments, however, his short game never left him.

"If I have one regret, it was a decision I made just prior to the Open at Oakland Hills," Runyan once said. "I had received a new putter at my shop and had used it in a round where I shot a 61. I decided to take that putter with me to Oakland Hills and leave my regular putter, which I had a lot of confidence with, back in California. It was the worst mistake I ever made. I putted horribly. While I believe I was the only player in the field who did not have a three-putt green, I didn't come close to putting up to my regular standards. I believe I finished fifth, but it could have been much better if only I'd had my old trusted putter. It was a hard lesson to learn."

BABE RUTH

Babe Ruth and Ty Cobb were fierce rivals on the ballfield and, as it happens, skilled golfers. The Babe was about a six-handicap who could blast drives with the same power that made him a legendary home-run hitter. Cobb, a nine-handicapper, lacked Ruth's power, and while he could shoot some good scores, his volcanic temper made him woefully inconsistent.

Still, they were passionate golfers and, even after they left baseball, remained two of the biggest names in all of sports. Of course, none of this was lost on Fred Corcoran, the most skillful golf promoter of his time—or any other time, for that matter. Over the course of his career, Corcoran was involved with both the PGA of America and the LPGA, got the World Cup off the ground, and was an agent for Sam Snead, Babe Zaharias, and Ted Williams.

In 1941, Corcoran convinced Ruth to challenge Cobb to a fifty-four-hole charity golf match for the "Ruth Cup." Cobb, who at fifty-four was six years older than Ruth, declined. Corcoran, not to be deterred, sent Cobb a telegram under Ruth's name and, for good measure, leaked it to some friendly writers.

"If you want to come out here and get your brains knocked out, come ahead. Signed, Babe Ruth."

Cobb, whose competitive fires hadn't banked with the passing of time, had no choice but to accept. The game was on.

The first eighteen was played before a huge gallery at the Commonwealth Country Club in West Newton, just outside Boston. Cobb was on his game and won, 3 & 2. After the match, he couldn't resist giving his old rival a jab, for the benefit of the local papers.

"The fat man is getting fatter," he said. "He looks out of balance, like an egg resting on two toothpicks."

Not for nothing was Ty Cobb the most despised man in baseball.

Ruth came back to win the second match, played at Fresh Meadow Country Club in Flushing, New York, setting up the third and final eighteen at Grosse Ile Country Club in Detroit. Cobb wasn't going to take any chances.

He hired Walter Hagen as his coach.

He hired the club's assistant pro as his caddie.

And on the boat trip across Lake Erie, he made sure Ruth's glass was always filled with scotch.

The next day dawned hot and humid. Ruth, nursing a horrific hangover, was nauseous on the first tee and didn't feel any better by the time they made the turn—in part because he was five strokes back and in part because Cobb blew smoke from a particularly odious cigar in his direction every chance he got.

On the back nine, Cobb offered Ruth a bet to help him save face.

"How much?" Ruth asked.

"How about $50,000?" Cobb said. "You name it."

153

Wisely, Ruth settled for less—a lot less—and Cobb closed him out, 3 & 2.

"I used to play with Babe Ruth in exhibitions," remembers Gene Sarazen. "Oh, he could hit that ball a mile, but he played Catholic golf—a cross here and a cross there."

GENE SARAZEN

Gene Sarazen made his final appearance in the British Open in 1973 and went out in style by making a hole in one on Troon's infamous "Postage Stamp" hole.

"Now that I've played my last round here in the Open, I know my old friends Walter Hagen, Bobby Jones, and Tommy Armour are up there in heaven waiting for me," he joked with the press. "I can hear them now—'C'mon, Gene, hurry up, we're on the tee.' Well, I've got news for them. They're going to have a long wait."

And they did. More than twenty-five years later, he was still as feisty as ever.

Throughout his career, Gene Sarazen was known for his strong opinions and his absolute delight in voicing them.

In 1926 he traveled to the Royal Montreal Golf Club for the Canadian Open. When the course was built, it was on the outskirts of the city but reachable by the local rail service. But as the city grew, it came to surround the course. Between the noise of city life and the railroad tracks that ran through the course, playing Royal Montreal's Dixie course could be a trying experience. Sarazen certainly found it so.

"This isn't a golf course," Sarazen fumed to the press. "It's like playing through a goddamned freight yard."

Gene Sarazen played in tournaments right through the Depression, although sometimes it was hardly worth the effort.

"I won a tournament in New York and was thrilled because that first-prize money was going to come in handy," Sarazen remembered. "After they had a big ceremony, the president of the club, who was a prominent banker in New York, handed me a check. I looked at it and it was blank. I asked him what the story was, and he said he was sorry but the club was broke. He did congratulate me on winning, though."

Gene Sarazen met British great Harry Vardon at the 1920 U.S. Open at Inverness, but only in passing. Vardon was one of the game's greatest players, and this was Sarazen's first major championship.

They were paired together at Sarazen's first British Open. Vardon hit first. When it was Sarazen's turn, he took the wind into account, but it never moved the smaller British ball.

"Will you look at that, the wind never touched that ball," Sarazen said to Vardon.

"No," Vardon said, "and the way you strike the ball, the wind won't affect it a bit."

Before he developed the sand wedge, Gene Sarazen—like most players of his era—struggled when he hit his ball into a bunker. In those days, they truly were hazards.

One day, while practicing his bunker shots, Sarazen asked a friend of Willie Anderson how the four-time U.S. Open champion played from the sand.

"He doesn't," the man said. "Willie is never in bunkers, and that's why he's won four U.S. Opens."

Sarazen's career paralleled the growth of golf around the world. He was an ambassador, traveling to the four corners of the Earth to play exhibitions and tournaments. It was a profitable learning experience for Sarazen.

"My first visit to Japan was unlike anything I'd ever experienced before," Sarazen recalled. "I was playing a match and I hit my ball into a bunker. I played it out, and after I walked out of the trap, I looked back and there were people in there measuring where my feet had been placed. I felt like a science project."

Sarazen was known as "Mr. Double Eagle" in Japan, which he always thought made him sound more like an Indian chief than a golfer. Of course, the reference was to his dramatic double eagle on the 15th hole during the final round of the 1935 Masters.

It was during a trip to Japan that he lost the 4-wood that he used to hit the historic shot.

"I think I may have given it away, but I'm not sure," Sarazen said. "Whatever happened to it, when the government found out it was missing, they had every policeman in the country looking for it. As far as I know, it was never found."

Sarazen and 1928 U.S. Open champion Johnny Farrell traveled through Europe on an exhibition tour. They traveled to Rome, the birthplace of Sarazen's parents, and at the request of the United States ambassador, they paid a call on Benito Mussolini, the country's dictator.

"When we arrived, I noticed a red carpet," Sarazen said. "I said to Johnny, 'See, they don't mind that I changed my name [from Saraceni]. They rolled out the red carpet for us.'"

The words were barely out of his mouth when workers began removing the carpet.

"We got there just after the Pope had left," Sarazen recalled, laughing.

Gene Sarazen won seven major championships and was the first person to win all four of the modern or professional majors. Clearly, he had talent, but more than anything else, he had a fierce desire to win and a competitive—even pugnacious—personality.

"Gene was the only player that ever intimidated me," recalls two-time PGA champion Paul Runyan, no shrinking violet himself. "Bob Jones didn't. Hagen didn't. Armour, Snead. None of them intimidated me. But I played Gene in my first PGA Championship and he thoroughly beat me. It wasn't just the way he played. He had an aura about him. I just never felt I could beat him—and a lot of other very good players felt that way, too."

"Back in the old days they didn't rope off the fairways, so the gallery would get out there and form a horseshoe behind you while you played," Sam Snead remembers. "I was playing a match against Gene one time. We had a huge gallery and they were kind of out of control. I outdrove Gene on this one hole, and after he hit, the gallery broke and ran so they could watch me play. This one guy ran right over Gene and knocked him to the ground. Gene got up and chased him down. He still had his club, and I thought he was going to kill the guy."

Gene Sarazen once gave Calvin Peete, a twelve-time winner on the Tour, a bit of advice that has stayed with him over the years.

"He told me to always remember that the trophies will tarnish and the money will be gone, but no one can take away your memories—not even the IRS," Peete said.

CHARLIE SIFFORD

Charlie Sifford, who helped integrate the PGA Tour and won the 1967 Hartford Open and 1969 Los Angeles Open, knew what he was getting into when he turned pro in 1948.

"In 1947, I talked to Jackie Robinson about my plans to try and play on the Tour," recalled Sifford, who also won twice on the Senior PGA Tour. "He looked me right in the eye and asked me if I was a quitter. I told him I wasn't.

"'Good,' he said. 'If you're a quitter, quit now, because you'll never make it.'"

"Jack Nicklaus's father, Charlie, was always very nice to me," Sifford remembered. "He owned some drugstores around Columbus [Ohio], and he always brought me some real nice cigars when he came to tournaments. One year I was playing with young Jackie in Akron. We were paired in the first two rounds. I shot a 64 in the first round. Jack shot a 63 in the second. After the round, I told Charlie, 'You know, you might have something here.'"

JAY SIGEL

Philadelphia's Jay Sigel was the dominant amateur of his generation. He won two U.S. Amateurs, a British Amateur, and three U.S. Mid-Amateurs. He captained two Walker Cup teams, played on nine Walker Cup and seven World Amateur teams, and won both the Bob Jones and Ben Hogan Awards from the United States Golf Association. Having built a successful insurance business, when he turned fifty he joined the Senior PGA Tour, where his fellow players voted him the 1994 Rookie of the Year.

Unlike a lot of players, Sigel isn't particularly superstitious. For example, 13 is his favorite number.

"I was born on November 13th," he explained. "My first hole in one came on the 13th hole on July 13th, and when I won the British Amateur, I became the 13th person to win both the British and U.S. Amateurs."

To take it one step further, when he won the 1997 Bruno's Memorial Classic, he played in group #13 on each of the last two days.

SAM SNEAD

Sam Snead is deeply respected by his fellow players, not only for his playing ability and his remarkable record but also for his knowledge of the golf swing. They often seek him out for advice.

"One time I was in an awful slump and happened to play a practice round with Sam," Raymond Floyd remembers. "When we finished, I said, 'Sam, I know there has to be a secret. There has to be something you know that I haven't figured out yet.' He kind of looked around, like he wanted to make sure there was no one who would overhear us. Then he said, 'Junior, you've got to turn. You've just got to make a good turn.'

"I said to him, 'That's it?'

" 'That's it, junior,' he said."

It's safe to say that Sam has taken to heart the old saying "A fool and his money are soon parted." And Sam is certainly no fool.

"Back when Sam started to make some money on tour, he bought a '36 Ford Roadster with a big Mercury engine and superchargers," remembers his good friend Bob Goalby, the 1968 Masters champion. "You can imagine the reaction when he roared into Hot Springs on a visit home. They'd probably never seen anything like that up in the Virginia mountains. His brother, Homer, fell in love with the car and badgered Sam to sell it to him. Finally, Sam agreed to sell it for $900. A few years ago he told me, 'You know, old Homer gave me $15 for a down payment and then he kind of forgot the rest— but I haven't.'"

On another occasion, he told Goalby about a loan he'd given former Masters and U.S. Open champion Ralph Guldahl.

"'Goldie and I won the Miami Four-Ball one time,'" Sam said. 'We got $1,600 each, but Goldie was getting married and he borrowed my $1,600 and gave me an IOU. Goldie was kind of a take-your-time kind of guy. I used to kid him that if he gave anyone a blood transfusion, they'd freeze to death. Sure enough, he never did pay me back.'

"And with that, Sam pulled the IOU out of his wallet," Goalby said, laughing. "He'd been carrying it around since about 1939."

Fred Corcoran, Sam's longtime agent, had a genius for coming up with schemes that would get press coverage to help promote golf and, of course, his clients. One time he floated a story that Sam and Sugar Ray Robinson were going to have a very interesting competition.

"Ray said he'd play me if I'd give him a stroke a hole," Sam remembered. "Then we'd go box five rounds and he'd spot me the first four. I said that would be okay if I could bring my wedge into the ring and break both his legs."

Sam Snead won a record eight Greater Greensboro Opens, but the sweetest win of the eight might have been the last one, in 1965, when he was fifty-two years old. In fact, he was within weeks of his fifty-third birthday, making him the oldest player to ever win a PGA Tour event. He and Raymond Floyd are the only players to win PGA Tour events in four different decades.

Sam was honored at a dinner prior to the start of play, and when a speaker mentioned how great it would be if Sam won that week, it got Sam thinking about his chances. But it was something else that got him grinding.

Sam heard that a player was complaining about Sam being in the field. He questioned why a player with no chance of winning was allowed to take up a spot in the field. That was all it took.

Sam not only won, but he won by five strokes over Billy Casper, Jack McGowan, and Phil Rodgers.

"Somebody asked that player later what he thought about my win," Sam said later, chuckling. "He said, 'I think I was wrong.'"

Of all the records that stand as testimonials to just how great a player Sam Snead was, here's a record that rarely gets mentioned: the number of course records he holds—a staggering 164.

CRAIG STADLER

No one ever accused Craig Stadler of being a colorless clone. Far from it. His displays of emotion are dazzling. His glorious mustache earned him the perfect nickname: The Walrus. His game combines pure power with a sublime touch around the greens—and writers know he's usually good for a quote or two.

♦

When Stadler was a kid growing up in San Diego, he was part of a group that took lessons from two-time PGA champion Paul Runyan. Years later, after Stadler had won a U.S. Amateur and twelve PGA Tour events, including the 1982 Masters, a writer asked Runyan about his early impressions of Stadler. Runyan said he thought Stadler was one of the shyest youngsters he'd ever seen.

Several years later, an interviewer asked Stadler about Runyan's assessment.

"Actually, I thought he would have said that he thought I had a bladder disease," Stadler said, laughing. "Paul is a sweetheart and a very good teacher, but sometimes I'd get confused when I tried to follow what he was telling me. Pretty soon every time he came down the line on the practice tee and was about to get to me, I'd tell him I had to go to the bathroom. I didn't want to hurt his feelings, but I didn't want to get any more confused, either."

Craig Stadler shot a 79 in the first round of the 1998 Masters. As he walked toward the clubhouse, a writer asked him what number he had in mind for Friday.

Now, one thing you should understand about Craig Stadler is that any answer to a question like that, at a time like that, is probably going to be fairly concise. This was no exception.

"Nine-thirty," said Stadler, not breaking his purposeful stride.

"Nine-thirty?" the writer asked.

"Yeah, the nine-thirty flight out of here tomorrow night," Stadler said.

Not quite. The next day Stadler went out and shot a 68 and made the cut by a comfortable three strokes.

STUDENT AFFAIRS

By the late 1800s, golf was just starting to become popular in the United States, particularly along the East Coast. New Haven, Connecticut, was no exception, and in 1895 the nine-hole New Haven Golf Club was built.

Not surprisingly, golf's charms weren't lost on the students at Yale, and soon the course became crowded with students who preferred keeping their eye on the ball instead of the books.

It wasn't long before this became too much for some of the members, not the least of whom was Yale professor Theodore S. Woolsey. Professor Woolsey apparently liked his students; he just didn't like them in large numbers at his club.

Faced with what he considered an unbearable situation, he did the only logical thing: he and some fellow members founded the New Haven Country Club in 1898, with the proviso that Yalies would be prohibited from trampling about the place except as guests—and then only occasionally.

There's no reason to feel too bad for the Sons of Yale, though. In 1926 they got their own course, the Yale Golf Club, designed by no less a figure than Charles Blair MacDonald, the winner of the first U.S. Amateur Championship.

LOUISE SUGGS

Louise Suggs established one of the most remarkable records in the history of women's golf.

Suggs, whose father was a former major-league pitcher and owner of a golf course, dominated the game as an amateur. She won both the U.S. and British Women's Amateurs, two Western Amateurs, and three North and South Amateurs.

The Georgia native turned pro in 1949 and made headlines by beating Babe Zaharias, the defending U.S. Women's Open champion, by a stunning 14 strokes, setting a championship record. She won the Women's Open again in 1952.

As impressive as her amateur career was, she was even more overpowering as a professional. She was one of the founders of the Ladies Professional Golf Association and served as the group's president from 1955 to 1957. She won fifty LPGA titles in all, including four Women's Western Opens and four Titleholders, both tournaments that were considered major championships at the time. She also won the 1957 LPGA Championship, was the leading money winner in 1953 and 1960, and won the Vare Trophy for the low scoring average in 1957. No less a figure than Ben Hogan argued that her swing and her game made the ideal model for other women golfers to try to emulate.

Suggs was nothing if not strong-willed.

She resented the attention the press lavished on Zaharias and didn't bother to try to hide her feelings.

In 1962, she was fined $25 for failing to play in a tournament in Milwaukee. LPGA officials claimed that she'd reneged on a commitment to play. She disagreed and immediately cut back her schedule to ten or fewer tournaments a year.

"It wasn't the money, it was the principle that mattered to Louise," said Betsy Rawls, the LPGA's president at the time of the controversy. "Louise was still at the top of her game at the time. It was one of the saddest moments in LPGA history."

SUPERSTITIONS

Occasionally rites or traditions evolve into superstitions. That's the case with David Duval, who, at the end of 1997, was the hottest golfer on the PGA Tour.

Duval had been one of America's top amateurs—a four-time All-American at Georgia Tech—but struggled early in his professional career. In 1993, he finally broke through with a win in the Nike Tour Championship at Pumpkin Ridge Country Club.

That night Duval and his uncle were celebrating in a cigar bar when they spotted a bottle of Louis XIII cognac. Now, this is a very rare cognac. Extremely rare, in fact. So rare that it comes in a Baccarat crystal bottle.

The bottle was so beautiful, they asked the bartender about it. He told them it cost $1,500, or $110 a shot. Well, since it's not every day you get your first win as a professional, they decided to spring for a couple of pops—then a couple more. Then the bartender told them that the bar gave the bottle to whoever bought the last shot.

They drained it.

It would be ninety-two more tournaments before Duval finally got his first win on the PGA Tour, at the 1997 Michelob Championship. As luck would have it, his uncle was there and they celebrated with another bottle of Louis XIII. It must have been a good-luck charm, because the following week Duval won again, and another Louis XIII went by the boards.

Two weeks later, Duval picked up the biggest win of his career, the Tour Championship, with its winner's purse of $720,000. It made 1997 a very good year for David Duval—and Louis XIII cognac.

"Long" Jim Barnes, who won two PGA Championships, a U.S. Open, and a British Open, didn't have many superstitions, but the one he had was a beauty.

Barnes would walk along the edge of the rough during a round, head down, searching for four-leaf clovers. If he found one, he'd pop it into his mouth and keep it there for the entire round.

Rick Acton, who plays on the Senior PGA Tour, was once disqualified from a tournament several years ago for mismarking his ball. Now he doesn't take any chances. He marks his ball with one of four rare coins: an 1863 Indian head penny, a 1900 dime, an 1899 Indian head penny, or an 1858 Flying Eagle.

"I mark the ball with the head pointing toward the hole, except when I have to move the mark to get it out of someone's line," Acton says. "Then I flip it over to remind me to move the ball back."

South Africa's Simon Hobday, who won the 1994 U.S. Senior Open, is a walking catalog of superstitions. For example, he used to have lucky and unlucky numbers on his golf balls, but it became too confusing. Now he simply lets his caddie decide what number is lucky that week.

It gets worse.

"I don't much favor the color green, so I won't use green tees," Hobday explained. "I also stay away from green clothes, but if I do wear something green, I make sure to wear at least one other piece of green clothing with it."

Then there's the matter of 13th holes.

"Bloody unlucky, those," he says. "They're usually good for a bogey or double bogey. If I make one of those, my caddie will hand me a new ball right away. Helps get the jinx off."

What about lucky coins?

"It's hard to say," Hobday joked. "I've never been able to keep one around long enough. I always lose them."

Then there is the matter of clothes. Back in his glory days, if Sam Snead played a good round, he'd try to wear the same shirt the next day.

Tiger Woods—a former Stanford Cardinal—always wears a red shirt if he's in contention on Sunday. He feels red gives him added strength and power. It certainly worked in the 1997 Masters.

Seve Ballesteros was just the opposite. When he came into the last round with a chance to win, his choice was navy-blue slacks and sweaters and white shirts. He felt the dark blue helped soothe his nerves and keep him calm under pressure.

WILLIAM HOWARD TAFT

President William Howard Taft was an enthusiastic golfer, but at three hundred–plus pounds, he was hardly a picture of poetry in motion. This is, after all, a man who once became stuck in a White House tub while taking a bath.

After his presidency, Taft taught law at Yale, and he frequently played at the New Haven Country Club. There, his regular caddie was a young man named Ray Brock, who went on to become the club's president.

Mr. Brock must have been a very sensitive young man, for the spectacle of the enormous former president struggling to tee his ball soon proved to be too much for him. He took over the task himself—one assumes to the considerable relief of a grateful Mr. Taft.

TEMPER, TEMPER

"People talk about my temper, but old Tom didn't have anything on Lefty Stackhouse," Tommy Bolt once recalled. "I may have thrown a club now and then, but I never ruined an entire set. One time, back in the old days when they had hickory shafts, Lefty came in from a round and burned his whole set. He just made a little bonfire for himself and torched them. Now, that is a temper."

$\bigcirc$

"Clayton Heafner was what you'd call a brooder," Sam Snead remembers. "He'd get something under his skin and it would fester. He'd think about it and think about it, and the more he did the madder he'd get. One time he was driving to a tournament at a course he didn't really like. Naturally, all that time in the car gave him a chance to work up a nice little rage. When he reached the course he told the tournament officials he was pulling out. When they asked him why, he didn't bother to make up an excuse. He just told them their course was a goat track and then stormed off. That earned Clayton a nice little fine from the PGA, but at least he got it off his chest."

JEROME TRAVERS

J erry Travers was one of the great American players in the early part of the twentieth century. From 1906 to 1915, he won four U.S. Amateurs and a U.S. Open—one of only five amateurs to win the Open.

To say that Travers marched to the beat of his own drummer is to put it mildly. In the years he was at the height of his game, he twice failed to enter the Amateur and he never entered the Open after his win in 1915.

Like Bob Jones, who retired from championship play at a young age, Travers all but quit serious competition while he was quite young—age twenty-eight. The difference was that Jones retired because he had won the Grand Slam and had nothing left to accomplish. No one is quite sure why Travers retired when he did.

The keys to Travers's success were his phenomenal putting and his uncanny ability to focus, to the exclusion of everything going on around him. Witness his match with Francis Ouimet in the finals of the 1914 U.S. Amateur at Ekwanok Country Club in Manchester, Vermont.

"I was fortunate enough to beat Jerry, 6 & 5, and after I putted out, I waited for Jerry to come over and congratulate me," Ouimet remembered. "Instead, he walked right past me, took his driver from his caddie, and walked off to the next tee. One of the officials ran after him and asked if he was planning to play the bye holes. 'Why,' Jerry asked, 'is the match over?'"

WALTER TRAVIS

Walter Travis was one of the game's greatest amateurs at the beginning of the 20th century. Between 1900 and 1904, he won three U.S. Amateurs and a British Amateur at a time when the amateur championships were every bit as prestigious as—and maybe even more so than—the respective opens. That Travis finished second in the 1902 U.S. Open at Garden City Golf Club on Long Island is all the more remarkable when you realize that he didn't even take up the game until he was thirty-five.

Travis, who was born in Australia but lived in America, could be difficult—to put it mildly. He didn't care whom he offended, and sometimes he seemed to go out of his way to annoy people. He was seldom without one of his truly nasty black cigars clenched tightly between his teeth. It's not clear what people found more irritating about Travis—his cigars or his personality.

Not surprisingly, then, Travis was a fierce competitor. Even his most vocal critics would give him that much. His win in the 1901 U.S. Amateur was not only one of his greatest triumphs but also one of his most nerve-racking.

The championship was played in Atlantic City, New Jersey, and Travis won the thirty-six-hole qualifying medal by three strokes. By the luck of the draw, however, he faced a difficult route to the finals.

He faced Charles Blair MacDonald—who could be equally difficult—early in the match-play rounds and managed to beat the winner of the first U.S. Amateur. In the semifinals he came up against the formidable Findlay Douglas. Douglas, who had won the U.S. Amateur in 1898 and had lost in the finals of the previous two championships, ranked with Travis as one of the premier amateurs at that time. The match figured to be a classic, and thousands of spectators came from all along the East Coast to watch it. They weren't disappointed.

The lead and momentum shifted back and forth between the two players until, at the end of thirty-six holes, the match was tied. Travis won on the second hole of sudden death.

The final promised to be every bit as tense, as Travis would face Chicago's Walter Egan, who had cruised to an 11 & 10 win in his semifinal. But the finals would have to wait. That evening, news came that President William McKinley, who had been shot eight days earlier, had died. The country went into an official state of mourning.

When the final was finally played a week later, Travis's competitive edge showed. He won easily, 5 & 4, in the longest U.S. Amateur championship in history.

It's only fitting, given his personality, that Walter Travis should have been at the center of one of the major rules differences between the United States Golf Association and the Royal & Ancient Golf Club of St. Andrews.

When Travis won the 1904 British Amateur at Royal St. George's, he used a Schenectady putter, which the R & A promptly deemed illegal because of its center-shaft design. The USGA, on the other hand, felt the putter was acceptable under their interpretation of the rules, setting up a conflict that wasn't resolved until 1951, when the two governing bodies met and adopted the uniform Rules of Golf.

⛳

Walter Travis was a keen judge of talent. At the 1916 U.S. Amateur at Merion, he closely watched the fourteen-year-old Bobby Jones in his third-round loss to the defending champion, Robert Gardner. After the round, a writer asked Travis what Jones needed to do to improve.

"Well, he can never improve his shots," Travis said. "But he has a great deal to learn about playing them, and when he does, he will be all but unbeatable."

Travis was right.

The rest is history.

⛳

Travis set a record by shooting rounds of 75-74—149 in the final two rounds of the 1902 U.S. Open at Garden City Golf Club. He finished in a tie for second place, six strokes behind Laurie Auchterlonie.

As an amateur, Travis was ineligible for his $100 prize money. Instead, he asked USGA officials to use $75 of the prize money for a trophy and give the remaining $25 to his playing companion, Alex Smith, for his "thoroughly sportsmanlike spirit throughout the championship."

⛳

A long with his ever-present cigar, Travis was known to take a drink now and then. In fact, he relished a good, stiff pop or two. Once, however, on the eve of an important tournament, he decided to give abstinence a try. It was a short-lived effort.

"I conceived the idea that my game would be improved if I stopped drinking and smoking, so I cut out both," he explained. "I found that while it made no difference in my long game, my work on the greens was nothing short of childish. I couldn't putt at all. I have never since allowed even golf to interfere with either my smoking or drinking."

Spoken like a true champion.

LEE TREVINO

Like many people gifted with a sharp sense of humor, Lee Trevino knows how to turn it into a weapon when it's called for. A classic case occurred at the 1984 PGA Championship at Shoal Creek in Birmingham, Alabama.

Two things should be noted here: first, Trevino's caddie, Herman Mitchell, is a large black man whom Trevino is enormously fond of and loyal to; and second, the tournament was played amid a swirl of racial controversy because Shoal Creek was unapologetically segregated.

At any rate, as Trevino and Mitchell were walking toward a tee, some genius in the gallery called out, "Hey, Lee, what do you feed your caddie?"

"Rednecks," Trevino called back, not breaking his stride, "and he's hungry."

Lee Trevino and Herman Mitchell were perfect for each other. They could joke with each other on the course and they could argue as well—although it was usually for public consumption.

"One day Herman and I were really going at it," Trevino recalled. "I was telling him that he couldn't caddie worth a damn, and he was telling me that I couldn't play. After I walked away, a woman asked Herman if it was always like this.

"'No, this is a good day,' Herman said."

Lee Trevino was staying at the home of a Mrs. Mayberry during the 1974 PGA Championship at Tanglewood Golf Club in Winston-Salem, North Carolina. One evening he was rummaging through her late husband's golf bag and found a Wilson blade putter that was exactly what he'd been searching for.

He asked her if he could buy it, but she couldn't bear to part with it for sentimental reasons. She did, however, tell him he could use it during the championship, and if he won, the putter was his.

The last thing Lee Trevino needed was yet another reason to win. It was like tossing gasoline on a fire. He went out and edged Jack Nicklaus by a stroke for his third major championship.

To go along with a handsome trophy and a nice check, he also got a putter that would serve him well for a long time to come.

L ee Trevino played pretty well from tee to green in the 1984 British Open at St. Andrews, but his putting was atrocious. His wife, Claudia—whose late father was a golf professional—thought she knew what the problem was but broached the matter with great diplomacy and a certain spousal delicacy.

"Honey, what kind of putter does Seve use?" she asked after watching Ballesteros edge Tom Watson for his second British Open title.

"A Ping," Trevino answered.

"And what kind of putter is Tom Watson using?" she asked sweetly.

"A Ping," Trevino replied.

"Oh," Claudia said. "And what kind of putter is Freddie Couples using?"

"He uses a Ping, too," Trevino answered.

"Can I ask you something else?" she asked.

"Sure," Trevino said.

"When are we going to get one?" she asked.

Pretty soon, as it turned out.

"We flew from Scotland to the Dutch Open," Trevino recalls. "I went into a pro shop and saw a Ping that looked pretty good to me. I bought it, banged it on the floor to flatten the lie, and went out and shot 13 under par to win the tournament. It worked like a charm."

In fact, it worked so well that a few weeks later Trevino, then forty-three, went out and won the PGA Championship at Shoal Creek by four strokes.

Claudia was credited with an assist.

When Jack Nicklaus was shooting a final-round 65 to win the 1986 Masters, no one watched more intently than his old rival, Lee Trevino.

"Claudia and I were in the airport waiting for our flight," Trevino remembers. "I was having a beer and watching the tournament on television. When Jack eagled 15, I told the bartender to forget about the beer and give me a double scotch. I mean, man, I never drink scotch, but I toasted Jack, the drink went right down, and I ordered another. When I called Jack to congratulate him, I told him I was happy for him but couldn't remember much about the rest of the round. I do remember that I was sick for about three days, though."

KEN VENTURI

One of the most popular players on the PGA Tour is Peter Jacobsen, in part because of his personality, sense of humor, and innate showmanship. In 1998, he and his band, "Jake Trout and the Flounders," released a CD. The Flounders included fellow pros Larry Rinker, Payne Stewart, and Mark Lye, and during one telecast CBS's Jim Nantz asked Ken Venturi whom he would have sung with back when he was playing the Tour.

"Frank Sinatra and Dean Martin," Venturi answered. "And I did."

In 1954, Ken Venturi was a soldier stationed in Salzburg, Austria. Over Christmas dinner, he was discussing his future with another fine young player, Tommy Jacobs. While playing the Tour was a possibility for both men, Venturi thought it was more likely he'd return to San Francisco, sell cars for Eddie Lowery, and remain an amateur.

Ten years later, when Venturi won the U.S. Open, Jacobs finished second by four strokes.

"If it couldn't have been me, I wish it was you," Venturi told Jacobs at the conclusion of the championship.

"No, Ken," said Jacobs. "It should have been you all along."

W hen Ken Venturi was thirteen years old, he saw Byron Nelson play golf and it made a huge impact on his life.

"I ran home and told my mother that I wanted to be just like Byron Nelson," he recalled.

Sure enough, a few years later he was introduced to Nelson, who became his mentor and one of his closest friends. Nelson not only helped shape Venturi's game but also the character that would see Venturi through the heights of victory and the depths of defeat.

V ince Lombardi, the legendary football coach of the Green Bay Packers, went to the last day of the 1964 U.S. Open. As he and his wife, Marie, were walking past the first green, they paused to watch Ken Venturi putt out. Venturi's putt hung on the edge of the cup, and the exhausted golfer stared at it, willing the ball into the hole. After a few seconds, it dropped.

"My God, his eyes are dead," said Lombardi. Instead of moving along to watch another group, Lombardi and his wife followed Venturi for the rest of his dramatic round.

For the rest of his coaching career, Lombardi would use the example of Venturi's courage and determination as a way to rally his teams.

TOM WEISKOPF

Tom Weiskopf was the first "Next Jack Nicklaus," which was probably inevitable given the fact that they were both born and raised in Ohio and played for Ohio State.

But even though Weiskopf was supremely talented, he never kidded himself about the comparisons with Nicklaus.

"Jack is two years older than me, and when we were at Ohio State, he was already the best golfer in the world," Weiskopf remembers. "In 1960, when Jack finished second at the U.S. Open as a twenty-year-old amateur, he was paired with Ben Hogan on the last day. Hogan said Jack should have won the Open by ten strokes, and he wasn't trying to jerk anyone around. That's how good Jack was."

While Weiskopf could match Jack's physical talent, he clearly understood the one thing that set the two men apart.

"Jack has this tremendous ability to set goals and then focus on accomplishing them," said Weiskopf. "I'll give you an example. In 1973, I won five tournaments in eight weeks, including the British Open. At the end of the year I felt like I was on top of the world, and I wanted to just enjoy the view. I promise you, if it was Jack, he would have said, 'Okay, I'm on top of the mountain. Where's the next mountain?'"

KATHY WHITWORTH

K athy Whitworth's eighty-eight victories make her the
most successful golfer in LPGA history. While she never
won the U.S. Women's Open, she won just about everything
else worth winning before winding down her playing career
and concentrating on teaching. In the end, the pressure of
competition and other people's expectations finally got to be
too much.

"I was talking about it with Ben Hogan one time," Whitworth recalled. "He said that the more you win, the easier
people think it is to win, while just the opposite is true. He
compared it to water dripping on a stone. You wouldn't think
that water could damage something as hard as a stone, but
eventually the water wears it down. That's how it was for me.
I just found I couldn't take the steady pressure any longer. I
knew it was time to get out."

THE WILD KINGDOM

Sam Snead grew up in the Back Creek Mountains of Virginia, where he learned to hunt and fish, passions that he would pursue all over the world. As a boy, his knowledge and skill for fishing was so great that he could literally catch trout—a notoriously skittish fish—by hand. Of course, this didn't always work out quite as he planned.

"When it was hot outside, the fish would get in there under the rocks to keep cool," Sam recalled. "You'd just kind of slide your hand in there real slow and grab a hold. You couldn't be quick or jerky, or they'd vamoose. One day I got in there and grabbed on to one and brought it out—but the son of a bitch was a water moccasin and it was a-fixin' to give old Sambo a bite. You never did see a snake fly as far and fast as that beauty did."

The Royal Sydney Golf Club—one of the finest courses in Australia—winds among sandhills and over a swampy area that was at one time condemned as unfit for buildings. Still, it was seemingly a perfect place for a golf course.

Seemingly, but not quite, perfect.

In 1931, a Royal Sydney member, D. J. Baley-McArthur, was out for a solitary round when he happened to hit his ball into what appeared to be a water-filled bunker. Mr. Baley-McArthur walked into the bunker to retrieve his ball and began to sink, first over his ankles, then his knees, then over his waist. He began to call frantically for help.

As luck would have it, a group of golfers on a nearby hole heard his shouts and raced to his rescue, just as he sank to his chest. They pulled him from the bunker, just moments before he would have sunk from sight.

Carnoustie, where Tommy Armour, Henry Cotton, Ben Hogan, Gary Player, and Tom Watson won British Opens, is one of the severest tests in golf. As Britain's John Morgan discovered in the 1968 British Open, sometimes the problems go beyond the course itself.

Morgan was addressing a shot on the 10th fairway when he felt a sharp pain. He looked down and saw a rat scurrying away, after taking a little bit of John Morgan with him as a souvenir of the Open championship.

Australia's Frank Phillips was playing a practice round prior to the 1958 Masters. Near the 6th green, he was startled by a blacksnake and killed it. After putting out, he stuck the snake into the cup and headed for the next tee.

As it turned out, Mike Souchak was playing in the group behind Phillips, and he was terrified by snakes. After holing his putt, he reached into the cup and got the shock of his life. He wouldn't pick his ball out of a cup for the rest of the round.

WIVES, LOVERS, AND
OTHER STRANGERS

In 1998, Michael Bonallack, the five-time British Amateur champion and current secretary of the Royal & Ancient Golf Club of St. Andrews, learned that he was going to be knighted. This meant that he would be known as Sir Michael and his wife, Angela, would be known as Lady Bonallack.

As is their wont, however, the Crown asked that Bonallack keep the honor a secret until it was announced to the press. Finally, on the eve of the announcement, Bonallack figured it was safe to tell his wife.

"Angela," he said. "As of tomorrow, you'll no longer be Mrs. Michael Bonallack."

To say Mrs. Bonallack was stunned would be putting it mildly.

"What's her name?" she asked.

Hubert Green was playing in the final round of the 1977 U.S. Open at Southern Hills in Tulsa when, with four holes to play, he was told that officials had received a threat on his life.

He was given three options: first, he could leave the course immediately and withdraw from the championship; second, he could request a suspension of play; or third, he could continue under a police guard. Green elected to play. Remarkably, he was one under par for the next three holes and then made a four-footer for bogey on 18 to edge Lou Graham by a stroke.

Later, writers asked him how he could remain so calm under such pressure.

"I just figured the threat came from an old girlfriend of mine," he joked.

A t four o'clock in the morning, just hours before he was to tee off in the first round of the 1935 Masters, Gene Sarazen was awakened from a sound sleep by a noise in his room. In the darkness, he saw a young woman move across the room.

No, it wasn't what you think.

The woman was after Sarazen's wallet, which was on the dresser. Sarazen sprang from his bed, grabbed a golf club, and chased the woman out of his room before she made her escape into the night.

If Sarazen was unnerved, he didn't show it. He went out and shot a 68 that could have easily been a 63 or better. He missed six putts of under seven feet and made only one putt longer than five feet. In the final round, he holed his famous 4-wood second shot on 15 for a double eagle then beat Craig Wood in a playoff to end a very eventful week.

The Westhampton course at The Country Club of Virginia was built in 1908. It is just a few miles from downtown Richmond, and a streetcar runs right to the clubhouse.

For many years, a successful insurance executive would be driven to his office by his wife. He'd kiss her good-bye, wait until she drove away, and then hop on the trolley and head for the course—where he would happily pass the day, playing golf, having lunch, and entertaining clients. At the close of the day, he'd hop the trolley in time to meet his wife for a ride home.

He was successful and happy. She was never the wiser. They had a long and successful marriage made, if not in heaven, at least on the 8:40 trolley.

In 1949, Ben Hogan and his wife, Valerie, were driving back to Fort Worth when their car was hit by a Greyhound bus. As the bus came out of the fog, Mrs. Hogan cried out: "Honey, he's going to hit us!"

Hogan instinctively threw himself across his wife, probably saving her life. He was badly injured in the crash, and many people thought he might not survive, let alone play competitive golf again.

When the ambulances finally arrived and pulled Hogan's mangled body from the wreckage for the trip to an El Paso hospital, Valerie Hogan kept her wits about her. Before climbing into an ambulance, she turned to one of the policemen on the scene.

"Please make sure you get Mr. Hogan's golf clubs," she said.

A rchie Compston was a fine player from England and a member of several Ryder Cup teams in the 1920s and '30s. Like many skilled golfers, he didn't come naturally to teaching when his playing days were over. He was often impatient, especially with beginners, and he didn't have what doctors refer to as a good bedside manner.

One day he was giving a lesson to a woman who was every bit as imperious as old Archie. Finally, she'd had enough of his attitude and hit him on the leg.

"You've finally bloody got it!" he yelled. "Now try it on the ball."

⛳

G olf, like life, is more complicated these days. Take this story from a public course in Atlanta.

A gentleman made a starting time for himself and his wife. He asked if there was a dress code and was told it was pretty informal. When they arrived at the course, it turned out he was a cross-dresser and was wearing a tennis dress.

It gets worse.

Apparently he must have looked pretty good in the dress, because as they prepared to hit, a man approached the two and asked if they'd mind if he joined them.

The cross-dresser turned and looked at the man.

"Not at all," he said, in a deep baritone.

⛳

TIGER WOODS

Tiger Woods's birthday is December 30, and as anyone who has a birthday that falls around the December holidays knows, it can be a mixed blessing. Sometimes parents have a tough time deciding what—and how many—gifts should be given.

In the Woods household, they came up with an interesting solution.

"Let's say that we decided to give Tiger a pair of shoes and a pair of socks," his father, Earl, once explained. "He'd get the right shoe and right sock for Christmas and the left shoe and left sock for his birthday. It helped keep up his sense of anticipation and excitement."

BABE ZAHARIAS

President Dwight D. Eisenhower was a passionate golfer and one of Babe Zaharias's biggest fans. One day he decided to call her and had the White House operators track her down. They finally found her at a hospital where Babe's friend, Peggy Kirk Bell, was having a baby.

"Tell Ike that Peggy's in labor and I can't come to the phone," the Babe said. "Get his number and tell him I'll call him back."

INDEX